ABOUT THE AUTHOR

Lou Ann Good, married and mother of four children, lives in Manheim, Pennsylvania. Now an executive secretary for a family counseling center, she has worked in several offices as a bookkeeper, receptionist, and switchboard operator. She is a Bible teacher in her church and coeditor of the church newsletter. Her articles have appeared in *Christian Living; Sprint; Power for Living; Teen Power; The Quiet Hour;* and other Christian journals.

Bible Readings

FOR
OFFICE
WORKERS

Bible Readings

FOR OFFICE WORKERS

Lou Ann Good

AUGSBURG Publishing House • Minneapolis

BIBLE READINGS FOR OFFICE WORKERS

Library of Congress Cataloging-in-Publication Data

Good, Lou Ann, 1946–
    BIBLE READINGS FOR OFFICE WORKERS.

    1. Clerks—Prayer-books and devotions—English.
I. Title.
BV4596.C54G66   1986   242'.68   87-1457
ISBN 0-8066-2250-4

Manufactured in the U.S.A.   APH 10-0693

1   2   3   4   5   6   7   8   9   0   1   2   3   4   5   6   7   8   9

For all those who implore,
"Lord, I need you in the office."

PREFACE

The expansion of banking, insurance, and
information industries in recent years has greatly
increased the number of office workers. According to a
recent report, 52% of the U.S. population now hold
white-collar jobs. The majority of these are within
office settings. The number of women entering the job
market has increased, and in this process many women
are experiencing more stress and competition. Both
men and women are faced with changing male-female
roles in the business world.

Despite all these changes, God's Word is relevant
for us today. *Bible Readings for Office Workers* is a
culmination of my own years of seeking to apply God's
Word in the business world. It by no means contains
all the answers. Instead, the meditations are intended
to point to Jesus, who does offer solutions for today's
problems. The closer we draw to Jesus, the more
fulfilled we are within ourselves. It then becomes a
natural response to take Jesus into every area of our

living. He will affect our careers, homes, and personal relationships.

When bombarded by the demands of high-pressure jobs, family responsibilities, and fatigue, we find it difficult to be sensitive to God's voice, but it is possible. This book is meant to help. Read the assigned Bible reading for each day. Ask God to make it relevant to your life. Use my written prayer and add your own heartfelt longings. Through these daily devotionals you will discover God's care, God's practical guidelines for success, and most of all God's love for you.

◼ TRUE FRIENDSHIP

Prov. 17:17-28:   "A friend loves at all times, and a brother is born for adversity" (v. 17).

I can't afford mistakes like this," Rhonda snapped as she slapped a purchase order on Diane's desk.

Diane stared in disbelief as she compared the item numbers with the quantities on the original copy. She couldn't believe she had made this major mistake, but the evidence lay before her—undeniable.

"I don't want this ever to happen again," Rhonda warned. Her eyes, cold as the stainless-steel pen she pointed toward Diane, threatened severe consequences.

Numbly, Diane nodded. To have made this mistake was humbling enough, but to be reprimanded in front of the whole office. . . .

A coworker's question interrupted Diane's agony. "Is that purchase order #6110?"

Diane nodded.

"I made that mistake," the woman said.

Relief, warm and comforting, surged through Diane. But greater than her relief was deep admiration for the woman who admitted her guilt when she could have remained silent. "This experience has taught me better than any sermon the value of treating others as I want to be treated," Diane said.

 Lord, let me be a true friend in times of joy and in times of distress.

Today extend kindness to a friend in need.

■ BUILDING RELATIONSHIPS

Micah 6:6-8:   "And what does the Lord require of you? To act justly and to love mercy and to walk humbly with your God" (v. 8).

Well, girl," Liz crowed, "last night I dined with Thomas, man of my dreams." She leaned forward confidentially. "And get a load of this—he makes $120,000 a year."

"Hmmm! You do have a way with the rich ones," Martha murmured. "Last month, it was Charlie building you your dream house. Before that it was. . . . "

But Liz waved her hand to silence Martha's memory. "Girl, this is different. This one has character." Liz laughed nervously, her earrings jerking as fast as her incessant chatter. "He lives in a fabulous bachelor pad."

"With his salary, he should," Martha said. "Where is it?"

"Scenic Hills," Liz's voice had dropped to a whisper.

Inwardly, Martha groaned. Established businessmen did not live in the Scenic Hills Apartments. Martha was sick of Liz's foolish bragging. But at that moment, Martha looked into her coworker's eyes. No longer did she see a 40-year-old divorcee, but a little girl, unloved, ignored, and desperately frightened. Martha recognized that Liz needed a friend to love and accept her for who she was, more than she needed someone to challenge her exaggerations.

 When I feel tempted to accuse, give me a heart, O Lord, that loves mercy.

Take time to build trusting relationships that need patience and love to develop.

■ THE PURSUIT OF EXCELLENCE

The gold-lettered nameplate revealed its shiny newness. "Mary Lou Sachs, President," it read. Mary Lou smiled with satisfaction. Now she would prove to the corporation's all-male board that she could perform better than any man.

No less than perfection was demanded from those under her. Strict office rules were enforced, with absolutely no loopholes. The pursuit of excellence nudged Mary Lou onward. The discipline paid off. Under Mary Lou's management, sales soared.

Months later, Mary Lou surveyed the office personnel. To her surprise she discovered unsmiling employees, wrapped in cocoons of tenseness, mechanically performing their jobs.

Eventually, Mary Lou recognized that the root of her employees' unhappiness was her own demanding attitude. Success had become more important to her than people. With the same diligence Mary Lou had shown to achieve financial profits, she now searched for answers to improve employee morale. She learned to listen, to praise, and to understand that all human error could not be avoided. Today, as a result of her own change of attitude, Mary Lou has happy, dedicated employees.

 May I always realize, O God, that people are far more important than my goals.

Express appreciation for each coworker's individual talents.

■ THE PRIVILEGE OF FORGIVING

Heb. 2:5-18:   ". . . so that by his death he might destroy him who holds the power of death—that is, the devil—and free those who all their lives were held in slavery by their fear of death" (vv. 14b-15).

Doug slammed the computer printer lid, swore at the copier machine, and glared at his coworkers. His mind was like the computer he operated. Press a few buttons on the terminal, and within seconds you had all the data that had ever been fed into the machine. Ask Doug a question, and all the rotten things that had happened in his life spewed out of his mouth.

Doug attended church. He knew that Jesus said we should forgive those who wrong us. That made Doug's life even more difficult. His anger extended toward God, who he thought demanded an impossible feat.

Then Doug started reading the Bible. He stumbled across an amazing truth in the book of Hebrews. "I found out I don't *need* to forgive," Doug said. Then he added with a grin, "I *get* to forgive."

Looking at the truth in that perspective shed a whole new light upon it. Doug realized that Jesus wasn't requiring something of him; he was giving Doug a choice, a way of escape from the emotions that hounded him.

How terrible life would be if we had no choice between forgiving or holding a grudge! Because Jesus destroyed the power of sin, we are set free.

 Lord, thank you for the power you provide for me to forgive those who have wronged me.

Today I will concentrate on Jesus, who offers a way of escape from my bondage to the past.

◼ SECRET SIN

Psalm 139:   "Search me, O God, and know my heart; test me and know my anxious thoughts. See if there is any offensive way in me, and lead me in the way everlasting" (vv. 23-24).

Thoughts of Jan occupied Greg's mind more than the trial-and-balance sheets before him. Jan would be the ideal wife, he thought, not like his present wife, preoccupied with her nursing supervisory position, blind to his own needs and the attention he craved.

What had begun as a friendly coworker relationship with Jan had grown into intimate sharing, nothing immoral yet, but the potential for that was growing. Greg knew he had to end the course of his thoughts before he was hopelessly entrapped.

Only when he attempted to restore his relationship with Jan into proper perspective did he realize the depth of his emotional involvement. As Scotch tape clings to paper, Greg clung to God, trusting God to lead his thoughts in purity.

Those first weeks were painful. His feeling for Jan was stronger than the belief that God would deliver him from the constant temptations. "But God is faithful," Greg says. "Today I am free. How great to know God's strength!"

 Lord, make me aware of dangers that can be avoided. Cause me to hear your warning signals.

What temptations do you personally find most troubling? Pray for God's guidance.

■ GOD'S UPDATE

Gen. 45:1-8:   "So then, it was not you who sent me here, but God" (v. 8).

Data-entry operators spend hours entering transactions in computer systems. The information accumulates but lies meaningless within the system until the files are updated. With the flick of a button the update process automatically applies the entered transactions to master files.

The process of updating files is a picture of God, who specializes in updating personal files. Joseph's life was an accumulation of disappointments with no visible purpose. He was falsely accused, rejected, separated from family and homeland, a pauper in prison, seemingly forsaken by God. Even his dreams were a mockery to the reality of his situation.

Then God updated Joseph's records, all his past experiences began to interface. The rejection of his brothers had brought him into the right location for future blessings. Joseph's past faithfulness in interpreting dreams in prison now provided his deliverance. Within hours of Joseph's release from prison he held the second highest position in Egypt. In time he experienced the reestablishment of family relationships, the fulfillment of his dreams, new prosperity, and the realization that God had directed his life's destiny from the beginning.

Lord, my life is like a puzzle, scattered pieces that will not fit together unless your hand touches them. Touch me, O God.

Make a list of the circumstances that intertwined to prepare you for the job in which you find fulfillment.

■ LETTERS OF REFLECTION

2 Cor. 3:1-18:   "You show that you are a letter
from Christ, . . . written not with ink but with the Spirit
of the living God, not on tablets of stone but on
tablets of human hearts" (v. 3).

Daphne finished typing the letter and held it up for
inspection. The print was indistinct. Each character
was two-toned, dark at the top, light at the bottom.

Daphne examined the typewriter for possible
defects. The cassette carbon ribbon was fresh, the
print pressure was adjusted correctly, everything
appeared adequate. The finished print, however, was
definitely blurred.

A serviceman suggested a new type-style disk to
replace the old one that had worn unevenly. After
Daphne inserted a new disk, she admired the clear,
sharp imprint of the letters.

As she compared the new copy with the inconsistent
print of the old letter, she wondered if her imprint on
life was clear. Was part of her life a clear testimony to
the Lord and the remainder an inconsistent blur? Just
that morning she had spoken about the joy God gives
and then went on to complain about the weather, her
job, and the economy. She determined that with God's
help she would become a more consistent letter, truly
reflecting the Spirit of Christ.

 Lord, it's me again, needing a fresh touch from
you so that others may read your message
more clearly.

**In your own words write a letter explaining how you
would persuade or dissuade others to respond to
God's call.**

■ ACTION VERSUS PRAYING

Josh. 7:1-12: "The Lord said to Joshua, 'Stand up! What are you doing down on your face?' " (v. 10).

At times God insists we act rather than pray. When the Israelites fought the battle of Ai, it should have been an easy victory for them. But the Israelites suffered defeat. In despair, Joshua and the Israelite elders tore their clothes and fell face down to the ground before the ark of the Lord, remaining there until evening.

God wasn't impressed. Instead God said, "Stand up, what are you doing on your face? Israel has sinned. Get rid of that sin. That is why you cannot defeat your enemies."

Today, many office workers respond to difficulties in a similar fashion. Loren, a computer programmer, was one of those. His boss had requested that he write a program to perform a specific function. It required much research, something Loren detested. Loren kept busy with other things and continually postponed the job. The inevitable happened. His boss did not forget. Loren was red-faced as he blabbered inadequate excuses for his delay.

Loren recalls, "I needed to face my own sin of procrastination. The answer to my problem was not prayer alone. Instead, it required digging up the information I needed to perform my job."

 Too often I blame my failures on you, God. Give me courage to deal with the sin in my life.

What steps can you take to improve your performance at work?

■ LEGAL DEDUCTIONS

Mal. 3:6-18:   "Will a man rob God? Yet you rob me" (v. 8).

Sarah compared the accounts-receivable checks with the invoices. Company terms required full payment within 30 days. If payment was made within 15 days, the customer was entitled to a 3% discount.

Many late-paying customers deducted the discount from the total amount due, even though they weren't entitled to it. These accounts required additional work for Sarah. Letters needed to be sent to customers requesting the full amount, and adjustments had to be made in recording the accounts receivable. As Sarah fumed over the tightfistedness of people, she heard God whisper in her spirit, "You're like that."

Sarah's eyes widened in disbelief as she considered that rebuke. Then she remembered. Last week her personal budget was tight. The most logical place to cut corners appeared to be her tithe.

Strange, how the customers looked so miserly in her sight, yet her own deductions from God's account seemed so logical and deserved.

 I'm stingy, Lord. Worse than that, I don't even want to become generous if it means a cut in my expense account. Still, I recognize your call to transform me. Here I am, Lord.

When you feel that you can't afford to give more, think about the many ways God has enriched your life.

19

◼ MISPLACED FAITH

Col. 2:6-23:   "So then, just as you received Christ Jesus as Lord, continue to live in him, rooted and built up in him, strengthened in the faith as you were taught, and overflowing with thankfulness" (vv. 6-7).

Everything had gone wrong. A dead car battery caused Shane to miss the conference meeting, an irate employee complained of unfair treatment, and an important labor-saving device that Shane had planned to incorporate was deemed unrealistic by the company president.

Shane breathed a long wearisome sigh. All this getting up early for Bible reading and prayer—where did it get him? No job advancement in sight, not even calm everyday living.

He had heard glowing testimonies of others who claimed everything worked out supernaturally when they had daily devotions with God. Shane felt bitter toward God, who he thought had given him a raw deal for his loyalty, and he envied others who were seemingly rewarded for their dedication.

Like Shane, many Christians believe God owes them a life of ease if they attend church, read the Bible, and pray. Instead, God says that just as we trusted Jesus to save us, by faith, we can trust him with each day's problems.

 I realize, Lord, that I can never be good enough to deserve your blessings, but I trust in your mercy and favor.

Examine your motives for praying and living for God. Are you attempting to pressure God into giving you something you desire, or are you responding in appreciation for God's love and daily care?

■ THE SECRET OF COPING

Mark 1:35-45:   "Very early in the morning, while it was still dark, Jesus got up, left the house and went off to a solitary place, where he prayed" (v. 35).

Despair. That was the feeling Kristen felt most often after a busy day in the office. She thought, "If being a secretary was my only role, I could cope, but it isn't. I'm a wife, a mother, a Christian, a Sunday school teacher, a neighbor."

Jesus, too, faced extreme demands on his time and his services. He had the responsibility of teaching 12 disciples. Multitudes of sick and needy pursued him. Enemies attempted to corner him with their clever questions. Jesus faced lack of sleep, privacy, and recreation. In spite of these restrictions, Jesus sought time alone to pray. From these times, he drew strength, peace, and trust.

If the Son of God needed these times in fellowship with God, how much more do we need them. As career persons in secular jobs, we may not easily find quality time with God. Communion with God isn't available in packaged computer programs with adjustable options. Yet, we soon discover that fellowship with God is a priority without which we cannot survive.

 Lord, quiet this hectic pace that orders my days. Sweep over my soul with the calmness of your Spirit.

Converse with God in the solitary hours and it will be easier to deal with pressures in the marketplaces of your life.

■ ORDINARY DAYS

Eccles. 2:17-26:   "A man can do nothing better than to eat and drink and find satisfaction in his work" (v. 24).

Ugh, what a boring, endless job!" Deb groaned.

Maureen looked up. "I love ordinary days," she said simply. "The smell of coffee, the click-click of typewriters."

Deb's eyes widened in amazement. "You're crazy, Maureen," she said.

"Not now," Maureen answered. Then she added softly, "But at one time I was diagnosed a schizophrenic. Living was a tormented nightmare. I lost the ability to perform even the simplest human function." Maureen paused, her memory replaying the agony of those months. Then she smiled, "But Jesus set me free. That's why I love ordinary days. I know the joy of being able to work."

Few of us have had Maureen's experience. If we did, that perspective would indeed enable us to appreciate mundane days much more. Most of us are like Deb. We crave excitement, action, and entertainment, but life is made up of routine days.

Because the majority of our time is spent performing daily tasks, the wisdom of Solomon declares that one of the highest rewards a person can attain is experiencing satisfaction in our everyday chores.

 Lord, let me be sensitive to the joy of ordinary days.

When you despair over the boring details your job demands, try thanking God for the security routines offer.

■ FINDING CONTENTMENT

Exodus 2:   "And Moses was content to dwell with the man" (v. 21 KJV).

Jenny slid back on her chair and surveyed the endless stacks of brochures that needed to be stuffed into envelopes. "I wasn't born to do this," Jenny cried inwardly. "This isn't what I want out of life."

Approximately 3500 years ago, Moses found himself in a similar dead-end situation. Well-educated in the courts of Pharaoh, Moses had attempted to deliver a fellow Hebrew from the tyranny of forced labor. But his intentions were misunderstood, and circumstances forced him to flee to Midian to escape the wrath of Pharaoh. For 40 years he dwelt in exile. Moses' talents were seemingly shelved during his seclusion.

In Exodus 2 we read that instead of being bitter, Moses accepted his situation and lived in contentment.

Like Moses, we are sometimes forced into desertlike places, barren of even dreams to carry us through the dryness. If we concentrate on the unpleasant things within our lives, they soon consume our every thought. To live through these times of unfulfillment we need to concentrate on the good, insignificant as it may seem at the time.

 Open my eyes, Lord, to see the good things in my job. Cause me to find joy in the simple things that surround me.

Search for the pluses your job offers and verbally express them to someone today.

■ OFFICE FLIRTING

Eph. 5:1-14:   "Nor should there be obscenity, foolish talk or coarse joking, which are out of place" (v. 4).

It began innocently. A silly joke, more absurd than immoral, had surfaced in the conversation between Jill and Larry. In the weeks following, they discovered that lighthearted flirting made the time go faster and brought some laughter into the dull routine of the accounting office. They weren't serious. After all, they were both happily married. As long as they didn't really mean it, how could it be wrong? Everyone did it.

The Bible stresses that not even a hint of sexual immorality or any kind of impurity should be mentioned among God's people. It instructs us that unwholesome talk should never come out of our mouths, but only what is helpful for building others up according to their needs.

Joking about immorality isn't something that makes us better persons. The media bombards us with suggestions that encourage the lowering of morals. Too little is said that encourages wholesome relationships, the sense of worth and integrity that God desires to place within us.

We cannot upgrade the world's conversations, but we can and are responsible to control our own speech.

 Holy Spirit, teach me wholesome creativity in my conversation. Let my words be upbuilding, for your name's sake.

Can you recall a situation when you were the victim of flippant remarks? What can you do to discourage unwholesome talk?

■ THE ACCUSER

James 3:7-12:   "With the tongue we praise our Lord and Father, and with it we curse men, who have been made in God's likeness" (v. 9).

Fifteen dollars," Chet whistled. "That was stolen on purpose. No one accidentally forgot to pay that amount of money." The money had been stolen from the lunchroom snack-money container, which was used on an honor system.

Whispered conversations of possible suspects invaded the office. Chet was positive it was Carol, the young divorceé with the sad, brown eyes who sat isolated from the others. Earlier that week, she had confided that she desperately needed money. Her ex-husband hadn't sent the support money for weeks, and with two small children, things were desperate.

Chet voiced his suspicions to a coworker, casting accusing glances in Carol's direction. She kept her head bent over the company ledger.

Later that week Chet discovered that second-shift shop personnel had been losing quarters in the soft-drink machines. Thinking the money belonged to the same vendor, they reimbursed themselves from the snack-box coins. Guilt and shame swept over Chet. His accusations that earlier seemed so convincing now looked foolish and sinful.

 O God of mercy, I who call myself by your name find it far too easy to accuse. Forgive me.

Words can hurt or heal, bring joy or sadness, build up or tear down. Today speak words of life to those you meet.

■ FACING DIFFICULTIES

Psalm 138:   "The Lord will fulfill his purpose for
me" (v. 8).

Jack's eyes blazed with anger. "You have ruined your
chances for advancement within this company by the
way you have handled this project," he accused
Stephanie as he shoved the report across his desk.

Stephanie knew that Jack considered her a threat. A
department-head position would soon be filled either
by Stephanie or Jack. Stephanie knew that he had
purposely withheld essential information.

Anger welled up within her. She wanted to
condemn him, run to the company president, and
expose the cover-up. Yet, she sensed the Holy Spirit
reminding her of Psalm 138. The Bible promises that
God will deliver us from the plots of enemies. God's
plan for us will be fulfilled in spite of opposition.
These verses became Stephanie's daily prayer. She
looked to God to defend her and trusted God to fulfill
his purpose for her.

It was difficult. For more than one year Stephanie
worked under Jack. She attempted to do her work
well, without resentment or revenge. Sensing an
uncompetitive spirit within Stephanie, Jack soon began
to rely on her. In time, Jack, himself, recommended
that Stephanie receive an advancement.

"That year was not wasted," Stephanie insists. "In
addition to the valuable lessons I learned in getting
along with others, I began to trust God."

Thank you, Lord, that you are my defense and
that you do indeed fulfill your plans for me.

Give an example of God's redemption in your life.

■ INCOMPETENCE

Num. 13:27-33:   "We should go up and take possession of the land, for we can certainly do it" (v. 30).

Computerized hospital billings are often challenged by irate patients who claim they have been charged for services not rendered. Every day Winnie is one of the hospital clerks who receives verbal abuse concerning the hospital's billing system. "People fail to realize that the hospital's billing system is very complex," Winnie complains. Hospital billings probably are more complex than most billings, but that is no excuse for sloppy bookkeeping.

Twelve Israelites were sent to spy out the promised land. Ten decided it was hopeless to attempt to enter the land of promise. "There are giants in the land," they complained. Two of the spies, Joshua and Caleb, recognized the giants, but they claimed, "Our God is able; we can do it."

In our jobs we sometimes face giants of frustrations and unresolved problems. If we dwell only on the difficulties that loom before us, we are defeated. But when we concentrate on the possibilities, the unlimited resources God provides, and take one step at a time to solve the problem, the giants retreat before us.

 Lord, your strength really does outweigh the giants in my life. Let me concentrate on your amazing strength.

When you are troubled by a problem, take some time in your busy schedule and give thanks for God's many blessings.

■ THE VALID PASSWORD

John 10:1-10:   "I am the gate; whoever enters through me will be saved" (v. 9).

Four teenagers illegally entered a school's computer system and tampered with the students' grades. These teenagers' actions triggered many other cases of computer fraud. To protect records from being obtained unlawfully, many companies require a security password entry. If an invalid password is used in a computer program, a warning buzzer sounds, and the screen flashes a message, "Invalid password; job cancelled."

Illegal tampering is not limited to computer entry. In John 10 Jesus tells of those who attempt to gain access to God through invalid means. There is only one way to approach God. Any other way is resorting to thievery and will not pass God's security system. All who desire access to God have the opportunity if they use God's valid password. That password is Jesus. There is power and authority in the name of Jesus.

Through trial-and-error methods computer buffs sometimes stumble onto a valid password that allows them access into the system. But in the spiritual world, that will never happen. If we ignore God's Word and attempt to pressure him into answering our prayers because we have abstained from sin or use any other method, our prayer requests are cancelled. It is because of Jesus that we may approach the throne of God.

 Thank you, Jesus, for enabling me to come boldly before God.

Contemplate the saving power of Jesus.

■ RELIABILITY

Matt. 21:28-32:   "Which of the two did what his father wanted?" (v. 31).

Whenever anyone in the office requests assistance, Jolyn gladly lays down her pen and tackles the project at hand. In the meantime, Jolyn's own work collects dust. Papers that should have been filed weeks earlier topple across her desk and onto the floor. The clutter doesn't bother Jolyn. But the backlog does interfere with the smooth flow of office work. Time and again, Jolyn's supervisor must issue ultimatums to force her to complete her duties.

Like Jolyn, we may impress some with our acceptance of additional duties, but if we are not completing our own job we are not reliable.

Jesus told the parable of two sons. One promised his father to complete a job, but did not do it. The other son initially rejected doing the work his father requested but later changed his mind and did it. "Which of the two did what his father wanted?" Jesus asked. Of course, we recognize it was the son who actually finished the task.

This Scripture verse implies that we should not promise to do something we do not complete. When accepting a position with a company, we agree to fulfill the responsibilities it entails. Assisting others is commendable, but our first responsibility is to complete the duties within our job descriptions.

 Lord, sometimes I'd rather do another's work. The variety is inviting. If possible, let me fit it in. But let me realize my responsibility is to complete my own tasks first.

Describe a reliable worker.

■ THE RIGHT PERSPECTIVE

Lam. 3:31-33:   "Though he brings grief, he will show compassion, so great is his unfailing love" (v. 32).

After graduating from college, Troy was offered a lucrative job as head computer programmer for a large corporation. The salary was substantial. His former classmates envied him.

Troy foresaw no problem in adapting to this position, but from the beginning things seemed stacked against him. Changes in company management swept in a new set of ground rules and company strategy. Management blamed Troy for computer breakdowns over which he had no control. Troy begged God for wisdom in performing his duties.

Finally, management informed Troy that he was not performing according to their expectations. His employment was terminated. "It was bad enough not to have a job," Troy said as he recalled that dark period of his life, "but worse was the total devastation I felt because I decided that God hadn't helped me. He had forsaken me."

Eventually Troy located an inside sales job. In retrospect, Troy views his past experience differently. "God was looking at the whole scope of my life and knew that my fulfillment would be much greater at my present job. I had been looking at only one short segment of my life, and so I didn't realize that God really was caring for me."

Lord, I am baffled when my plans do not progress. Let me trust in your wisdom.

Give some examples of how God sees beyond our limited perspective.

WILLPOWER VERSUS GOD POWER

Rom. 8:5-14:   "We have an obligation—but it is not to the sinful nature, to live according to it. For if you live according to the sinful nature, you will die; but if by the Spirit you put to death the misdeeds of the body, you will live" (vv. 12-13).

Lauren was involved with a married man. The man was deeply in debt and had several children. Because Lauren loved him, she gave her paycheck to him with the hope that they could build a life together someday.

Lauren is a captive of her emotions. She does not realize that she does indeed have a choice. She can choose to do the right thing, not because she feels like it, but in obedience to God's standard. God invites Lauren and all of us to rely on him for strength. For the Christian, this is not willpower but God power.

It's true that when we are in the middle of a temptation, emotions seem stronger than God's power. Often temptation isn't a fleeting feeling but a bombardment of wrong emotions. Wrong emotions are those that go against the truth of God's Word.

God's power becomes active in our lives when we look past our emotions and see the One who is greater than our emotions. Because God is greater, God will give us strength to break the power of this stronghold. It may be weeks or even months, but God promises that when we act in faith, feelings that line up with God's Word will eventually follow.

 Lord, teach me to live by truth rather than emotion.

Talk with a friend about willpower and God's power in your life.

■ EFFECTIVE COMMUNICATION

1 Cor. 2:1-5:   "When I came to you, brothers, I did not come with eloquence or superior wisdom as I proclaimed to you the testimony about God" (v. 1).

When Rachel became Mr. Smith's executive secretary, she threw away all the form letters. She told Mr. Smith that business associates are friends. "If your letters have a friendly tone, they will be more effective," she said.

Mr. Smith viewed Rachel's new style of letter writing with dubious eyes. Her business letters sounded like personal notes. Yet her letters activated a response. They paid off in increased sales.

Rachel also believes that when she talks to others about God, it is even more important to maintain a friendly, normal style of speaking. No stiff archaic terminology for her. Standard church phrases like "hungry for God," "saved," and "washed in the blood of the lamb," often sound meaningless to nonchurchgoers. Yet the concepts behind these terms are still true and can be conveyed without compromise in clear, easy-to-understand sentences. It is important not to worry so much about the precise words but to concentrate on developing a friendly relationship with others. Out of that friendship, a natural opportunity to share about Jesus in a relaxed, down-to-earth style will develop.

 Jesus, I love you so much. Teach me how to convey your greatness to others.

Today begin to let your friendly manner enhance your opportunities to share your faith with others.

■ THE BREATH OF LIFE

Ezek. 37:1-10:   "So I prophesied as he commanded me, and breath entered them; they came to life and stood up on their feet—a vast army" (v. 10).

Ashley is young. An ethereal beauty surrounds her. Her dreams lie before her untarnished by life's disappointments. She is hardly like Ezekiel's valley of dry bones. Yet every time her friend Cher reads the Scripture referring to Ezekiel's vision, she thinks of Ashley. Why? Because Ashley is dead—spiritually dead of any sensitivity to God.

One day Cher had tried to tell Ashley that God gave the Ten Commandments not as restrictions but out of God's love. Ashley's eyes grew hard. "The Ten Commandments are unrealistic and outdated!" she said.

In situations like these, we realize how inadequate our words are to convey spiritual truth to others. Persuasive speech alone cannot cause people to seek God.

Ezekiel faced this in his vision of the dry bones. Death reigned in that valley. Nevertheless, God told Ezekiel to prophesy to the bones. Ezekiel spoke the Word of God; the bones joined together and flesh covered them, yet they remained devoid of life. They needed the breath of God to enter them. God's breath did enter them, and they stood up a living, vast army for God.

 God, my words are empty, useless, unless you breathe life into the listeners. Breathe on them, that they may truly live.

Contemplate on a time of spiritual dryness when you were refreshed by the Spirit.

■ RECOGNIZING OUR LIMITATIONS

Exod. 18:13-23:   "The work is too heavy for you; you cannot handle it alone" (v. 18).

The computer command-station flashed a message to change forms on the printer. Louetta yanked the printout forms from the paper compartment and replaced them with a box of invoices. She adjusted the position of the invoices, pounded the start button, dashed to the command station, recorded the change, pushed the enter button, and rushed back to the printer. A screeching noise caused Louetta to groan. She had forgotten to adjust the pressure. Now a black smear, the result of too much pressure, darkened the white invoice copy.

"I feel like that printer," Louetta muttered as she adjusted the pressure dial. "Too much pressure makes me feel like shrieking. And my whole life is becoming a messy blob from too much work."

Louetta knew that to operate efficiently she needed to be relieved of some of the pressure caused by too much responsibility. But to admit that to her superiors seemed like a sign of weakness.

Like Moses, we want to fulfill our specific responsibilities. Yet there are times when we consistently use our time wisely and are efficient, but there is not enough time to do all that is required. If we force ourselves to continue our hectic pace, we will wear ourselves out.

 Lord, I cannot do everything. I know it. Now let me be humble enough to admit that truth to others.

If you are overworked discuss this problem with a friend.

■ CREATIVITY

Genesis 1:   "God saw all that he had made, and it was very good" (v. 31).

Our God is a creative God. Since we are formed in God's likeness, we have a creative drive within us. Creativity covers a wide range of possibilities. It can be expressed in artistic talent or an original idea to improve our job.

If our creative drive cannot be used in our daily jobs, we need to find another outlet to satisfy it. That is difficult. As full-time employees, responsibilities and lack of time handicap us.

Linford discovered a way to combat the time problem. He said, "I always enjoyed woodworking, but after work, performing house chores, and playing with the kids, I had no spare time. A growing feeling, which Linford describes as sort of a poverty within, forced him to find a time slot that would not interfere with his family's needs.

He discovered the satisfaction he achieves by getting up one hour earlier is worth the lack of sleep. "I actually have more energy because I'm finding time to do something I enjoy. I don't feel guilty that I'm not with the family—they're still asleep. Plus, I made an amazing discovery: it isn't any harder to get up earlier."

 Lord, I believe that the poverty of spirit I sometimes feel is a lack of fulfilling the creative drive you placed within me.

Experiment for one week: set your alarm one hour earlier and do something you enjoy.

■ BETTER METHODS

Jer. 31:31-33:   "I will put my law in their minds and write it on their hearts. I will be their God, and they will be my people" (v. 33).

Ann, the new office manager, was bursting with innovative ideas and time-saving methods. She had installed a computer system that eliminated the need for the ledgers that Norma had kept so painstakingly.

Norma nodded solemnly when Ann informed her that her bookkeeping methods were obsolete. As soon as Ann left Norma's office, Norma pulled out the ledger and continued to post the day's transactions. She was certain the old way was best.

Many view change as upsetting. The systematic order we have established in our duties spells security. Yet it is fortunate for us that change has developed in many areas of our lives. The greatest of all these changes was initiated by God. During Old Testament times God's people were guided by laws written on tablets of stone, but the mere establishment of the law did not produce obedience in the hearts of the people.

In his compassion God instituted a change: he promised he would write his laws on the hearts and minds of his people. That is exactly how God directs us today. God has placed the Holy Spirit within us. God's Spirit constantly nudges us onward in obedience to God.

 God, change is so scary. I cry out for the security of the past. Yet, again and again, I notice the positive side of change.

What changes have you made this week? Have you felt God's Spirit directing you?

■ EMPTY WALLETS

Hag. 1:2-11:   "You have planted much, but have harvested little. You eat, but never have enough. You drink, but never have your fill. You put on clothes, but are not warm. You earn wages, only to put them in a purse with holes in it" (v. 6).

When Andrea assumed ownership of Harrison Company, maximum profits became her top priority. She had faith only in her own skills and hard work. God was someone up there whom Andrea intended to learn to know better—someday, after her business was established, after her dream house was built. For now, Andrea decided, God could wait.

Andrea had her goals mapped out: a one-year plan, a five-year plan, and a ten-year plan. She attained her goal the first year. Yet there was not enough money for Andrea to relax her hectic pace. The figures proved she ought to be farther ahead financially, but she always needed more money. "It's like my bank account has a bottomless hole," she complained.

Andrea's comment echoes the sentiments of the prophet Haggai. Through this prophet God reprimanded his people: "You work so hard to take care of yourself. The more you get the more you need. It is never enough. Why? Because your top priority is to satisfy your own desires. Each of you is so busy taking care of yourself that you forget about serving me."

God desires to have top priority in our lives.

 God, forgive me when my selfishness gets out of control. Cause me to return to my first love— you.

Pray for a friend who serves God.

■ DOUBLE-DUTY ROLES

Jonah 3:1-10:   "When God saw what they did and how they turned from their evil ways, he had compassion and did not bring upon them the destruction he had threatened" (v. 10).

Adam works for an office supply company. Adam works both as a telephone salesman and as a collection manager for past-due accounts.

Studies show that a low-pitched, businesslike voice produces a higher percentage rate of results when making collection calls. Likewise, a cheerful voice that shows personal interest in the caller results in increased sales. Adam, therefore, changes the sound of his voice over the telephone in response to the type of call he is handling.

One day a caller asked the switchboard operator to first let him speak with Adam in the collections department and then with the Adam in the sales department. The switchboard operator informed the caller that Adam was only one person. The caller was incredulous. He insisted, "I spoke with both of them before. I'm sure you have two Adams, because they sound totally different from each other." Merely by changing the sound of our voice, we can be mistaken for two separate individuals.

God fills two different roles. God is a God of judgment who sometimes needs to issue ultimatums to those who live in sin. God is also a God of compassion, not willing to inflict punishment.

 God, let me be quick to hear your voice and to obey.

When preconceived ideas have blocked out God's true message for you, seek God's forgiveness.

■ SEXUAL HARASSMENT

Titus 1:10-16: "To the pure, all things are pure, but to those who are corrupted and do not believe, nothing is pure. In fact, both their minds and consciences are corrupted" (v. 15).

Hi, Love." The sound of Phillip's voice caused Sue to freeze momentarily. She detested Phillip's boldness, his excuses to touch her hands when she handed him office paperwork, his lingering smiles.

Her own smiles were distant as she attempted to keep their conversation on the business at hand. Sue believed that if Phillip were treated with businesslike respect, he would respond in kind. Her work demanded that she keep close proximity with Phillip, but she did not want to cause a scene by making an issue of his advances.

If Phillip sensed Sue's coldness, it did not daunt his familiar greetings, his many suggestions.

One morning, Phillip attempted to hug Sue. "Keep your hands off of me," she ordered.

"I was only joking," Phillip answered with a nonchalant shrug. "Can't you take a joke?"

"I was only joking," is a standard cliché that many persons hide their true motives behind. They attempt to turn the finger of guilt away from themselves by making the other person feel foolish. The Bible warns us that in the last days there will be many rebellious people, mere talkers and deceivers who must be silenced. Today's Bible reading instructs us to rebuke them sharply.

 God, grant me boldness in those situations that demand it.

How can you discourage sexual harassment?

■ CONFLICTING MESSAGES

1 Peter 3:7-12: " . . . so that nothing will hinder your prayers" (v. 7).

George slammed down the telephone receiver. "Wives!" he snapped. "Don't ever get married," he advised Tom, his assistant supervisor. "My wife orders me around like her servant. 'Please pick up a carton of milk on the way home. Get the lawn mower fixed,'" George mimicked. "I'm sick of it."

He pounded the computer keys in order to reach a file maintenance screen. Instead of releasing the program, the screen flashed a message: "conflicting program in action; job cancelled." When too many computer terminals are used to add and subtract from the identical files at the same time, the computer cannot decipher the commands, because the messages conflict with each other.

George knew the task he was about to perform was aborted by the conflicting jobs. But he did not know that his attitudes toward his wife cancelled any prayers he might make. The Bible reading for today warns us that our prayers can be hindered by our attitudes and actions toward others. In spite of our wrong actions, God remains capable of answering our prayers, but he urges us to keep lines of communication open.

If your prayers are not answered, ask God to search your heart and show you anything you did that was displeasing. If God shows you anything, confess it. That clears your line of communication with God and enables God to answer your prayers.

 God, cleanse my attitudes toward others.

How can you choose to be attentive to the needs of others?

■ COMPARISON

John 21:18-22:   "Jesus answered, 'If I want him
to remain alive until I return, what is that to you? You
must follow me' " (v. 22).

Six months ago, Brad had left Fran for another
woman. The helplessness and devastation that had first
overwhelmed her was growing fainter. Fortunately,
Fran had been able to find a reliable day-care center
and a job as an insurance underwriter. Life was
beginning to be enjoyable again.

Rene swung her Corvette into the parking space
beside Fran, jumped out of the car, and pushed her
sunglasses atop her head. "Today is payday—another
check to blow at Winslows," she called.

Fran felt a twinge of jealousy. Rene always blew her
paychecks. Her mother baby-sat Rene's children and
cleaned her house free of charge. Rene's husband was
an executive and a devoted father.

Since the beginning of the world, human nature has
fallen captive to the sin of comparison. We want
fairness and equality. When Jesus requested that Peter
feed his sheep, Peter felt honored. Then he turned
and saw John. Peter questioned, "How does his future
compare with mine?"

Jesus answered, "What does it matter? Your
obedience to me is the important issue. You need not
consider the circumstances of others."

 Jesus, cleanse me of my compulsion to
compare my life with others. Let me rejoice in
the plans you have for me.

Contemplate the gifts God has bestowed on you.

■ OFFICE CHRISTMAS PARTY

Psalm 4: "You have filled my heart with greater joy than when their grain and new wine abound" (v. 7).

The Christmas party at Megan's office offered free drinks, gourmet food, and a night of unrestrained behavior.

Megan didn't expect God to speak to her that night. After all, God had seemed strangely silent despite her frantic pleas for direction these past months. Yet that night, in spite of the band's frenzied beat, Megan sensed God speaking to her. "Look around you," she sensed God whisper. Megan noticed the office gang. Their eyes shone with unusual brightness. Loud, ringing laughter punctuated their carefree banter. They looked happy, free of worry, fears, and inhibitions. "I give greater joy than this," Megan felt God say.

Megan knew that was true, but she did not feel God's joy. *Why was God's joy so evasive?* she wondered.

For the office personnel to have reached their relaxed state, they had needed to drink in total abandonment. If Megan desired to be filled with the joy of the Lord, she too, needed to drink—not the counterfeit wine that the world offered, but the living water that God offered. She needed to drink it freely, until she could relinquish her doubts and trust God's guidance in total abandonment.

 Fill my cup, Lord. Quench this thirsting of my soul.

Do you place all your trust in God's guidance? How does your faith influence your behavior at parties?

■ WORD POWER

Rev. 12:10-12:   "They overcame him by the blood of the Lamb and by the word of their testimony" (v. 11).

William, a customer-service representative, spends much of his time conversing with potential customers. William believes it is important to know how he sounds to the people he deals with each day. He declares, "My tone of voice, inflection, speed, and enunciation all convey a message to those who listen to me." By listening to himself, he has developed a convincing voice. William practices his speeches when he drives to work each morning. While driving, he places his finger firmly in one of his ears and speaks. He claims that closing one ear quiets the vibrations in his head and enables him to hear how he really sounds to others. "It works the same as a tape recorder," William insists. By practicing this exercise, William has developed a clear, emphatic speaking voice.

If it is important to know how we sound to others, it is even more essential to be aware of the message we convey to others regarding our relationship with God.

We cannot force persons to respond to the call of God, but the testimony of our life can influence others to seek God. The Bible teaches that the power of Satan in peoples' lives is broken by the combination of our testimony and the blood of Jesus.

 Lord, it is mind-boggling to realize the effect our words have on others. Let my speech be consistent with your message.

How can you improve your speaking ability?

■ WHAT IF

2 Tim. 1:7-10:   "For God did not give us a spirit
of timidity, but a spirit of power, of love, and of self-
discipline" (v. 7).

Jane drew a deep breath. "Know what the supervisor
said about you yesterday?" she asked.

Mark shook his head.

Jane smiled, a cool, condescending smile. "He said
he didn't think you were handling those reports
properly."

Mark feigned a humorous reply, but inside, Jane's
insinuating remark tore him apart. Mark had been
certain to research carefully, to check and recheck the
statistics.

When Mark returned to his project of preparing the
reports, his mind swarmed with confusing thoughts.
What if the reports were inadequate? What if he failed
to include essential information? The frantic what-ifs
destroyed his earlier feeling of competence and tore
any previous constructive ideas to shreds.

Fear blocks clear thinking. It kills faith, destroys
confidence, and fills us with depression. In its most
acute stages, it paralyzes action and destroys us.

Victory over fear begins by recognizing the source of
fear. The scripture reading today emphasizes that God
is not the author of fear or timidity. Through prayer
and concentrating on the task at hand, the what-ifs
that cloud our thoughts are pushed away.

 Dear God, grant me power over the fear that
envelops me.

Try to build the confidence of a coworker.

■ FRINGE BENEFITS

Ps. 103:1-18:   "Praise the Lord, O my soul, and forget not all his benefits" (v. 2).

Jack frowned as he glanced at the optometrist's bill. "I didn't realize glasses are so expensive," he remarked to Kevin. "It completely blows my budget. No eating out for me this month."

Kevin looked puzzled. "Aren't you going to submit your bill for company reimbursement?" he asked.

"Hey," Jack exclaimed. "I forgot. That is a company benefit."

Many people forget that God, too, offers benefits along with a plan of salvation. The Bible reading for today mentions 19 benefits for those who trust in God. More are mentioned throughout the Bible.

Today, many employees consider fringe benefits as necessary as their paychecks. Jobs are sometimes secured or relinquished depending on the benefits available.

During economic difficulties, some companies cut benefits or impose limitations on them. But God promises benefits that are from everlasting to everlasting. One can't find a more complete benefit package in any corporation. Examine them and see for yourself.

 It is good of you, God, to offer so many provisions for my care. Thank you.

Memorize the Bible verse.

■ COMPETITION

Gal. 5:13-18:   "If you keep on biting and
devouring each other, watch out or you will be
destroyed by each other" (v. 15).

Greta was not a supervisor, but that didn't hinder her
self-imposed position of bossing others. She believed
she could do everything better than anyone else. In
the bookkeeping department advice spewed from her
mouth each day. Others' mistakes never escaped her
attention, and she made sure that everyone knew
about them.

Greta's constant faultfinding intimidated others and
caused competition and tension within the office. Her
coworkers felt they needed to constantly defend or
justify their actions. The continuous conflict between
Greta and others was detrimental to the office
atmosphere. Employees were irritable and full of
revenge.

Many offices have an arrogant and domineering
person like Greta. It is easy to despise and even hate
persons like her. God admonishes us that that type of
reaction will destroy us. "Live by the Spirit," he says,
and you will not yield to revenge. To live by the Spirit
is to be continually aware of Christ within us. When
we concentrate on Jesus, our thoughts are not on the
injustices we suffer from those around us. His
presence makes all the difference in our reactions. He
enables us to love those who criticize us.

 Lord, let me be conscious of your abiding
presence, free from the fear of others and what
they might think of me.

Give an example of God's loving presence.

■ UNAPPLIED CREDIT

Rom. 4:18-24: "God will credit righteousness—for us who believe in him who raised Jesus our Lord from the dead" (v. 24).

Monday morning Shawn kicked his briefcase beneath his desk and sagged wearily into his office chair. He had failed again. He hadn't prayed enough, read the Bible enough, or even loved his family properly this past weekend. As he scanned the trial balance sheets that listed all the customers with past due balances, he noticed that Charleston Company's account was 120 days overdue. Before Shawn called Charleston Company to inform them that their account would be sent for collection, he checked their files and discovered they had an unapplied credit that was adequate to cover their overdue invoice.

Shawn does not realize it, but he, too, has an unapplied credit. His spiritual account with God has a deposit of righteousness within it that is ample to cover all of his failures. Jesus gives us "right standing" before a holy God. The goodness of Jesus' character becomes ours when we put our faith in him.

Like Shawn, many of us see all we should become and the debts we have accumulated from our past failures. We forget that God has extended credit that is inexhaustible and available to all.

 God, I'm tired of seeing my failures and imperfections. Today let me see myself through your eyes—perfect, just as if I'd never sinned— all because of Jesus.

When you feel overwhelmed by your own expectations, consider the generous credit line God offers.

■ SELECT YOUR THOUGHTS

2 Cor. 10:3-6:   "We demolish arguments and every pretension that sets itself up against the knowledge of God, and we take captive every thought to make it obedient to Christ" (v. 5).

Anne flaunted an air of superiority over all in the office. From her viewpoint, her work and her children were faultless. Her home, car, and wardrobe were meant to be impressive, not serviceable.

The morning Sarah heard that Anne lost her job, she rejoiced. "Good!" she thought. "It's time she gets knocked down a rung or two." As Sarah prepared a recap of the day's business transactions, she felt a nudge of the Holy Spirit convicting her of her lack of compassion for Anne. "Lord," Sarah prayed, "how can I love you and think such awful thoughts about Anne?"

Many thoughts enter our minds. Thoughts from the Holy Spirit encourage a closer relationship with God. In an attempt to override the thoughts God inspires, Satan drops his thoughts into our minds. Although we cannot always control the thoughts that flash through our minds, we can choose those we concentrate on, those that are in accordance with God's Word.

Just as Sarah needs a firm understanding of what she is looking for in order to select relevant statistics and ignore those that are not essential for her recap information, we need to understand God's standards in order to accept or reject the thoughts that bombard us.

 Jesus, conform my thoughts into obedience to you.

When you are tempted to criticize, concentrate on positive thoughts.

■ DESTINED FOR SUCCESS

Rom. 8:37-39:   "No, in all these things we are
more than conquerors through him who loved us"
(v. 37).

As purchasing agent, Walt scouted the market for the
best computer system for his office. Walt noticed that
price wars raged within the computer industries. Walt
said, "I didn't doubt that there would be an industry
shakedown. The market could not support many
companies that continued to operate on a marginal
profit."

Time proved Walt's prediction right. Many computer
companies have failed. Walt wanted to make sure that
he bought from a company that survived the
shakedown. Future service and compatible software
was as important as the computer itself.

In business, in games and in war, we all want to
come out on top. We cannot always forecast the
future, but God's Word does promise ultimate victory
for those who put their trust in God.

Whether we like it or not, we are all involved in a
battle between good and evil. The Word promises we
shall triumph over evil. We may not win all the
battles, but we will win the war. Why? Because Jesus
is victor. Through him we are victors over all that
seeks to destroy our faith. Nothing can separate us
from his love.

 Jesus, it is great to experience victory. It is
even greater to know you.

**Have you ever doubted God's promise of victory?
Learn a message of hope. Memorize today's Bible
verse.**

■ FASHION ME BEAUTIFUL

1 Peter 3:1-6:   "Your beauty . . . should be that of your inner self, the unfading beauty of a gentle and quiet spirit, which is of great worth in God's sight" (vv. 3-4).

The working men and women today are bombarded with advice on the proper image necessary to produce the right impression. "Dress for success, and you will be successful," we are advised. "Wear the right colors for your skin tone. Choose fine accessories with care to achieve the total look." The list of advice grows longer, and to follow it all we run the risk of being obsessed with our appearance.

It is true that tailored suits and well-cut hair styles can influence self-confidence and put us at ease. But even more important than outward appearance is the biblical injunction that beauty should not come from valuable jewelry or costly apparel. Lasting happiness, contentment, compassion, and hope do not stem from an extensive wardrobe. Instead, the presence of God within us makes us beautiful with inward qualities. These qualities are developed from a love relationship with God.

The finest clothing wears out, skin wrinkles, and expensive jewelry becomes outdated, but the beauty of a man or woman who is sensitive to the voice of God, gentle in compassion, is of great value in God's sight.

 God, fashion me beautiful with a sensitivity toward you. Clothe me with inner beauty.

Finances cannot limit the availability of God's wardrobe for each of us. When you dress for success, consider your inward qualities.

■ CHOOSE TODAY

Josh. 24:14-24: "Choose for yourselves this day whom you will serve" (v. 15a).

A rival company offered Margaret an executive position. Margaret wrestled with the pros and cons each company offered. She shook her head in despair. "They seem equal in opportunity and in benefits."

Eventually, Margaret decided the rival company had more potential for growth because of their upper-management policies. After all the years of convincing others why her company was better than the other, Margaret found it difficult to change loyalties. To be successful in her new position, Margaret could not hang on to her old ideas that this company was inferior. She needed to support her new company.

Each of us has a choice to make: will we live for God, or will we live for ourselves? Joshua challenged the people of Israel to live wholeheartedly for the Lord. It involved completely ridding themselves of all that would hinder their relationship with God. He reminded them that God is a jealous God, not willing to share his loyalty with other gods. "Don't make a half-hearted decision and believe you can serve God," Joshua warned them. "Choose this day."

Joshua, himself, was not influenced by the consensus of the people. Before they made their final decision, Joshua declared, "As for me and my household, we will serve the Lord" (v. 15b).

 I choose to serve you, O Lord. Whether my friends or family serve you or not, my heart is fixed: I will serve the Lord.

Life forces us to make many decisions. Today make the choice to serve God.

■ EMPTY WORDS

Mal. 2:13-17:   "You have wearied the Lord with your words" (v. 17).

Baker Corporation, a complex of comfortable plush offices, was filled with junior executives who relentlessly pursued their way to the top office. Richard was one of them.

Then inflation hit. Sales dropped. Costs increased. In typical corporation style, top company officials met behind closed doors to discuss cost-cutting programs. It was then that Richard had a firsthand view of the brutality that can be a part of big business. The executives reminded others of the need to sacrifice out of loyalty to the company, but their words belied their own selfish ambitions. Richard grew weary of the endless egotistical discussions that offered no viable solution to the difficulties of the company.

God, too, grows weary of words that only pretend faith and commitment to God, words that sound so right and spiritual when underneath are attitudes of contempt toward God and God's commandments. God is wearied by impressive acts paraded before others and prayers that are bribes.

Our attitudes convey our messages to God more clearly than our actual words. Therefore, we come to God, seeking grace and aid.

 God, let me live what I profess. Let me be transparent in my life both before you and others.

When you selfishly pursue your own desires, contemplate the message you convey to others and to God.

■ REBUILDING FROM THE RUBBLE

Neh. 6:1-9:   "They were all trying to frighten us,
thinking, 'Their hands will get too weak for the work,
and it will not be completed.' But I prayed, 'Now
strengthen my hands' " (v. 9).

The office operation was in disarray, and Heidi was
somehow expected to straighten it. She had been
hired to replace the office manager responsible for the
mess.

She employed every ounce of concentration to
delegate order in general office procedures. The office
staff resented the changes and complained that office
policy showed partiality to a favored few. Heidi wished
her employees would show more understanding of her
plight. If she could first concentrate on correcting past
accounting procedures, then she could more
adequately deal with personnel issues.

Nehemiah faced serious opposition when he began
to rebuild the wall of Jerusalem, which had been
ravaged by war. Some mocked and ridiculed his efforts
and accused him of treason. Those who assisted in the
rebuilding became frustrated by the rubble and the
demands of providing food, shelter, and protection for
their families. This drained their strength and
threatened to defeat the rebuilding.

Nehemiah met every challenge. He implored God
to give him wisdom in meeting every problem. God
did. The wall was rebuilt.

 Lord, grant me, your servant success.
Establish the work of my hands.

**When the demands of your job are overwhelming,
remember that God can provide insight and strength.**

■ WHO ARE YOU?

Rom. 8:31-35:   "What, then, shall we say in response to this? If God is for us, who can be against us?" (v. 31).

Let me speak to the man in charge!" Mr. Baker bellowed, glaring at Sonja Harris. Sonja swallowed uncomfortably, trying to choose a convincing response to this disgruntled client's challenge. His cunning manner and ruthless rejection of her as a person caused her to waver in indecision.

Then Mr. Potterbaum, the company president, opened her office door, "Good morning, Mr. Baker," he cordially greeted him. "You will find Miss Harris to be most helpful in solving your problems. She is our top consultant when dealing with sticky issues and has the ultimate authority for any and all decisions."

New confidence surged through Sonja as she faced Mr. Baker. She gained an inner resourcefulness to face her client with decisiveness. In response, Mr. Baker became a docile, willing recipient of her suggestions.

In our spiritual journey we sometimes face opposition that confuses us. We lose our sense of direction. We feel our insufficiency. The writer of Romans reminds us that God is for us. If God gave his one and only Son to die for us, will he abandon us now? "No!" the Bible declares. Jesus is at the right hand of God claiming our victory. If God is with us, nothing can destroy us.

 Jesus, flood me with the realization of who I am, because I'm yours.

What need or problem concerns you most? How could you work with God to take charge of the situation?

■ TRUTH PREVAILS

Gen. 39:6-20:   "And though she spoke to Joseph day after day, he refused to go to bed with her or even be with her" (v. 10).

Jed," his supervisor whispered as she draped her arms around him, "you're so neat."

Jed disengaged himself from Sheila's embrace. "Sheila," he replied, "I'm married. To pursue a relationship with you would be wrong."

"Oh, Jed," she pouted. "Life is too short not to enjoy it, and we could have lots of fun together."

Jed's rejection of Sheila's behavior did not discourage her. Instead, her coy flirting increased, and her demands became more insistent. One day, Jed warned her, "If you continue to try to touch me, I will report your behavior."

Sheila merely smiled. "He'll never believe you. I'll see to that." And she did. Jed was told, "It's your word against hers. There weren't any witnesses."

Joseph, too, was an innocent victim of a scheming woman. He was innocent of any charges brought against him by Pharaoh's wife, but he lost his job, his reputation was tarnished, and he was thrown into prison. This seemed like a poor repayment for one who remained loyal to high standards. But Joseph's life did not end in prison. In time, God rewarded Joseph for his faithfulness.

 God, defend the innocent. Strengthen your people with purity.

Remember that God promises to defend and reward, yet at times you must wait for God to act on your behalf.

■ DECISION MAKING

Psalm 16:   "I will praise the Lord, who counsels me; even at night my heart instructs me" (v. 7).

Jan's Copier Service was being edged out of the market by other larger, better-known franchises in the area. In desperation, Jan sought a consulting firm for advice on how to turn her business around. The consultants searched past and present records. They checked out the surrounding market and the competitors' edge. With their findings typed on sheaves of paper, the consultants gathered around the oak conference table with their suggestions. Possibilities were numerous, but always laced with warnings and the uncertainty of the future.

When the room grew quiet, Jan realized the ultimate decision was still hers to make. Jan didn't know which direction the economy would swing, the strategy of her competition, nor the future market trends.

Certain elements are known only to the One who holds the future. God promises to counsel us. If we ask for guidance, God will provide it.

In Jan's case, lack of capital to expand or to advertise widely was a form of God instructing her. Her personality and the personal interest and touch she had to offer were pluses to explore. Jan began to capitalize on that aspect. She personally called on prospective customers, and she inserted positive notes with each order. Today, Jan's Copier Service is a bustling business. Jan credits God for instructing her.

 Gracious Shepherd, lead me. Help me find your way.

Trust in God's counsel.

■ CALL IT WHAT IT IS

2 Sam. 12:1-13:   "Then David said to Nathan, 'I have sinned against the Lord' " (v. 13).

I have sinned," David admitted. That statement has a shocking bluntness to it. We don't like the word *sin*. It sounds more acceptable to our ears and to the ears of others to say, "I have made a mistake," or "I failed."

King David didn't minimize his sin. He didn't say, "I have sinned," and then add phrases like, "But it is my parents' fault," or, "Others do worse things," or, "I have been under too much pressure." Instead, David confessed his fault and recognized that God had every right to punish him.

Many of our failures, recurring problems, and mistakes are labeled sin by God. Only by calling sin by its real name will we begin to deal with it the way it needs to be dealt with—ruthlessly. Too often we circle aimlessly around the possible reasons we failed. We hide behind the excuse that we are a victim of circumstance. We complain that in a moment of weakness we succumbed.

Our usefulness to God isn't destroyed because we sin, but our usefulness to God is wiped out when we refuse to repent and call it what it is—sin.

God hasn't changed. He still abhors sin and asks for repentance. In God's compassion, God also offers forgiveness, cleansing, and mercy so that we can continue living with joy.

 I have sinned, O God. Wash me, and I shall be clean.

Ask for God's forgiveness and you will be forgiven.

■ FACING FAILURE

Ps. 37:23-28:   "Though he stumble, he will not fall, for the Lord upholds him with his hand" (v. 24).

Brandon had a flair for new ideas that captured attention. After developing a product superior to that on the market, Brandon launched a new business. The company flourished immediately. "Around us, newspapers reported that 65% of new businesses fail in the first five years," Brandon said. "We were hailed as a prime example that new businesses can make it. Then the bottom dropped out. Overextended credit, coupled with a similar product at a lower price introduced by our competitor, forced us out.

"I thought I'd die," Brandon confessed. "The dollar loss was nothing compared to my loss of face within the community. Everywhere I turned, they knew. I was stripped of self-esteem. I had failed."

It was the most forlorn experience of Brandon's life. At the same time, he began to feel that God had not abandoned him. "God was with me, encouraging me, whispering hope in the recesses of my mind. I gained new inner strength that I had never known possible," Brandon recalls.

The next year Brandon began another business, and he learned from his previous failure. Experience taught him more than he would have learned from others. But most important, Brandon insists, "I learned that God places an amazing amount of courage within us when we most need it."

 Lord, lift up my heart that I may lift up my head. Turn my mourning into joy.

How can you learn from failure?

■ WHEN YOUR BEST EFFORTS FAIL

James 1:2-8:   "If any of you lacks wisdom, he should ask God, who gives generously to all without finding fault, and it will be given to him" (v. 5).

According to this stock status report, we should have 125 extension hoses on hand," Carol said, pointing at the inventory printout. "But we don't have any." Because all inventory transactions were handled in Laura's department, Carol held her responsible.

Laura checked the transactions quantities and searched orders and invoices, but she could not discover the reason for the discrepancies. It was a baffling problem with no solution in sight. In desperation, Laura asked God for wisdom as she continued a diligent search for the errors.

That day Laura overheard a conversation by two department heads. From their comments Laura realized that through a misunderstanding of the intricacies of the computer system, they were giving her erroneous information to feed into the system. A simple explanation of the process solved the problems.

God's answers do not haphazardly drop from the sky, but God does promise insight for those who request guidance. Sometimes our best efforts fail. Things don't progress as planned. Remember that God, who knows and understands all complexities, is able to impart wisdom to us.

 Lord, illuminate my mind that I might understand.

Is anything too hard for God? If God made you, the universe, and all within it, can God not grant you wisdom?

■ SPECIAL DAYS

Luke 1:46-55:   "My soul praises the Lord and my spirit rejoices in God my Savior" (vv. 46-47).

Let's have lunch together today," Mr. Moore, owner of the Equipment Company, suggested to Jerry.

Jerry warily agreed. He knew the lunches with Mr. Moore were not leisurely times of relaxation, but were interspersed with plenty of timesaving pointers and advice on how to reach company goals.

Whatever Mr. Moore had in mind, he was saving for the end, Jerry thought, as they were finishing their pie and coffee. During the whole lunch Mr. Moore had not made one suggestion or request, but had complimented Jerry for his fine performance as office manager.

Mr. Moore sipped the last of his coffee, then pulled out an envelope and handed it to Jerry. It held a large check. Mr. Moore smiled. "I just wanted to express how valuable your performance is to our company, how much I appreciate you. This isn't a bonus, profit share, or payment for any other service. It is simply a thank-you for all the times you hung in there when things were tough."

Just as we enjoy being complimented, God, too, likes it when we express our appreciation for the wonderful things God has done for us. We are blessed when we spend time with God, free of requests, complaints, or demanding interruptions, a time of giving thanks and praise to God.

 Lord, I love the world you made, my family, and the job you've arranged for me. But most of all, I love you.

Squeeze more beauty from the moments of today.

■ MARGINAL CREDIT RISKS

Acts 9:1-19:   "I have heard many reports about this man and all the harm he has done to your saints in Jerusalem" (v. 13).

Trident Company is a bad risk," Jill, the credit manager, insisted. "All the reports show that they are late in payment."

"But think of the potential profit involved if they can make it," the sales manager argued.

Jill shook her head. "What is a $120,000 sale if you can't collect payment?" she asked. "I have gathered a financial analysis of their assets and liabilities. Trident Company is bad news."

Many years ago God gave a man who was a poor spiritual risk a new beginning. Saul had threatened the Christians of his day. He persecuted them night and day and caused havoc in the early church. No one was feared more than Saul. Saul deserved God's judgment for his cruel deeds, but God looked beyond Saul's past history and saw who he could become. God took a risk by confronting Saul on the road to Damascus and requesting his loyalty.

Saul, renamed Paul, didn't disappoint God. He gained a reputation as one of the most staunch followers of our Lord. Through him the gospel was carried to many nations, kings, and authorities. Today we read his epistles, and our understanding of Jesus is enhanced.

 Lord, thank you that you look beyond my past failures and see your dream for me.

Talk to a friend about risk taking.

61

■ LEARNING FROM CRITICS

Prov. 28:12-23:   "He who rebukes a man will in the end gain more favor than he who has a flattering tongue" (v. 23).

Bartman's customer-service representatives are required to participate in verbal class presentations in order to learn how to handle dissatisfied customers. After in-service training, Lynn's outstanding presentation brought an audience ovation. Everyone clapped except Dee, a fellow trainee. "You mispronounced criteria," she snapped. "And," she added, "everyone can tell you're from the South. 'Do y'all have a pamphlet?' "

Dee's derogatory comments whined in Lynn's mind for many months. Consequently, Lynn made a conscious effort to pronounce her words properly. She corrected colloquial idioms to conform with acceptable usage.

"Dee may have had ulterior motives when she criticized me," Lynn states, "but today I owe a lot to her. Much of my success in public speaking belongs to Dee. Because she was bold enough to criticize my speech, I have not made the same mistakes again."

Proverbs offer us much wisdom in human relationships. Although criticism may hurt at the time, if it moves us to take corrective measures, it can help us toward future achievements.

 Lord, enable me to accept negative comments and learn from them.

Don't allow criticism to become a personal rejection. Incorporate it into personal improvement.

■ DEALING WITH HOSTILITY

Matt. 22:15-22:   "Then the Pharisees went out and laid plans to trap him in his words" (v. 15).

An incredulous look spread across Mr. Jones' face as he repeated Carol's answer in mocking tones. "You have worked here one year and you can't tell me our average monthly budget?"

Carol flushed. Mr. Jones always asked her questions with the cocky assurance that she would not know the answer.

"How can you project an efficient company image if the figures aren't on the tip of your tongue?" he asked, continuing to needle her. "What do you do in your spare time? You should be studying company financial records, like I do."

Carol sighed. How could she make this bachelor understand that with two small children she didn't have spare time to do things she had no interest in pursuing? Their goals were different. Why couldn't they accept each other as they were instead of trying to change each other? Carol wondered.

Jesus also faced those who desired to expose him as a fool to the crowds that followed him. Sometimes he ignored their questions. Other times he asked questions of his own or confronted them with their evil intents.

Today, we face similar situations that require us to deal with hostility. We need God's insight to handle each incident with wisdom.

 God of all wisdom, teach me when to speak and what to say.

How are confrontations handled in your office?

■ SOURCE OF SECURITY

Ps. 118:5-11:   "It is better to take refuge in the Lord than to trust in man" (v. 8).

Two months earlier Pamela had sat in the company president's office. The president assured Pamela, "Your future with our company is absolutely guaranteed. Your skills and your initiative are invaluable to us."

Then the unthinkable happened. "Our bank was sold to another national bank. It was a complete shock to me, a young executive, climbing the ladder of success," Pamela admits.

The merger required fewer personnel. Pamela's position was eliminated. "My security was shattered. Only then did I realize how much I had trusted in my job and how little faith I had established in God as my provider," Pamela said.

Pamela had confidence in a guaranteed income, not in Christ. Like Pamela, we all need to realize that although God usually provides jobs for needed income, the job is not our true source of security. Jobs are only tools God uses. God's providential care is not limited to our particular job. Businesses fail. The economy fluctuates, but God's care for us remains stable, a secure foundation in troublesome times.

 O Lord, my provider, thank you that unemployment, inflation, and economical instability cannot separate me from your love and care.

Is your job an important source of security?

■ SENSITIVITY

Heb. 6:1-12: "God is not unjust; he will not forget your work and the love you have shown him as you have helped his people and continue to help them" (v. 10).

One afternoon, Mrs. Leffler, the supervisor of the secretarial pool, surveyed Rose's desk. "Rose," she reprimanded, "you have the messiest desk I ever saw."

In an effort to joke about it, Rose quipped, "Psychiatrists claim a neat desk is a sign of mental illness."

Mrs. Leffler's eyes hardened. "Face it, Rose, you are disorganized. Get your act together—today."

Her parting rebuke burned in Rose's thoughts. How dare Mrs. Leffler accuse her of sloppiness? "I'm overworked," Rose fretted. "I'm the one who accepts all the additional duties that no one else will bother doing. Because I don't get nasty, everyone throws spur-of-the-moment work on my desk. It isn't fair!" Rose stormed inwardly. Rose knew all the little things she did each day that required much more time than her supervisor realized.

Fortunately, God always knows all the details and circumstances that make up our life. He is always just. He understands our weaknesses and our limitations better than we ourselves understand them. We may not have a compassionate boss, but we are blessed to have a compassionate God.

 Lord, let me be more sensitive to the injustices others suffer and less sensitive to my own.

Although supervisors may not give us the credit due us, God always rewards us. What reward could be better?

■ HELPFUL CRITICISM

Matt. 23:27-39:   "O Jerusalem, Jerusalem, you who kill the prophets and stone those sent to you, how often I have longed to gather your children together, as a hen gathers her chicks under her wings, but you were not willing" (v. 37).

Sometimes executives must criticize. It's part of their job. Harsh, tactless criticism can hurt an employee's ego, but watered-down criticism can fail to remedy the problem.

At times God, too, needs to criticize us. His criticism is just, to the point, and given in love. If we accept his reprimands, he offers promise for the future, hope, and security.

Matthew 23 brims with Jesus' disgust at the hypocrisies of the Pharisees. He pointed out their inconsistent lives and begged them to turn from their deceit. Jesus made a poignant plea that he might gather his people to himself, to love them, give them a better life, and protect them.

Too often our response is identical to the Pharisees. We will not allow Jesus to do his work in our lives, because in our pride we believe we can succeed alone, and we don't want to relinquish our own desires and goals. But God still desires to gather us to himself. He longs to give us a life free from guilt, failure, and wrong attitudes.

 Jesus, don't let me block out your love with my wall of resentment. Open my heart to receive your forgiveness and love.

Don't allow criticism to smolder and build resentment within you.

■ BURNOUT

1 Kings 19:3-18:   "He came to a broom tree, sat down under it and prayed he might die. 'I have had enough, Lord,' he said" (v. 4).

Burnout is a new term for an ancient malady. Elijah, a great prophet of God who astounded thousands with the power of God, experienced burnout. Elijah witnessed the miracle of God sending fire from heaven to prove God's power over the idols of Baal.

Following Elijah's promise, God sent rain for the first time after a three-year drought.

Furious at the slaughter of her false prophets, Queen Jezebel vowed death to Elijah. He had faced threats before and survived. He had been instrumental in many displays of God's great power. But now, Elijah ran for his life. Exhausted, disappointed, Elijah begged God to let him die.

Elijah slept until an angel of the Lord awakened him and fed him. "What are you doing here?" God asked Elijah. In typical burnout response, Elijah answered, "I am the only one left, and now they are trying to kill me too" (v. 10).

God didn't argue. A mighty wind, an earthquake, and fire followed, but Elijah failed to see God in those mighty phenomena. Then through a gentle whisper, the Lord gave Elijah direction. He told of 7000 believers who had not bowed to Baal. From the Lord's direction, Elijah regained strength to continue living.

 Lord, I'm tired, disillusioned with living. Let me hear your still, small voice, O Lord.

When you experience burnout at work, what influences your recovery?

■ KEEPING CONTRACTS

1 Kings 21:   "Have you noticed how Ahab has humbled himself before me? Because he has humbled himself, I will not bring this disaster in his day" (v. 29).

Swanson Company owed Harper Electric $10,000. When Harper Electric attempted to collect this past-due account, Swanson Company had an excuse. "Our customer didn't pay us, so we can't pay you for the product," they complained. "When our customer pays us, we will pay you."

Harper Electric replied, "When you accepted our service, you contracted for payment on our terms, which are 30 days. We expect to be paid now."

In business and in personal life, many people blame their failure to live up to their promises on another's wrongdoing. King Ahab found it unpleasant to take the blame for a situation his wicked wife had instigated, but in the final analysis Ahab was as guilty as his wife. While Ahab had sulked because he could not purchase a vineyard he coveted, his wife schemed a murderous revenge in order to seize the vineyard. Through the prophet Elijah, God confronted Ahab for his murder of an innocent man and his other sins. King Ahab admitted his sin. He repented, fasted, and sought God. In response to Ahab's humility, God lessened King Ahab's deserved punishment.

 God, forgive me for my excuses and my searching for a scapegoat for my shortcomings. Teach me to accept responsibility for my actions.

Consider this statement: "Admitting guilt is not the end of a situation, but a new beginning."

■ THE LURE OF RICHES

Num. 22:21-35:   "I have come here to oppose you because your path is a reckless one before me" (v. 32).

Balaam, a prophet of God, was summoned by King Balak. "Help us," King Balak cried. "We are terrified of the Israelites. This horde is going to lick up everything around us, as an ox licks up the grass of the field. Come and put a curse on the Israelites so I will be able to defeat them."

Balaam knew the Israelites were God's chosen people, and he knew they were destined to possess the land. Now he faced a dilemma. Balak had offered him rewards if Balaam would curse the Israelites. How desperately he craved the riches and prestige that could be his by granting Balak's request! As God's prophet, he could not contradict God's command.

Balaam decided to accompany his guests to meet King Balak. God saw that Balaam was on a reckless path, and he sent an angel to stop him.

The lure of wealth had weakened Balaam's stand for God. Today, we are often enticed by the lure of profit or prestige to compromise our living for God. God has given us guidelines and standards to obey. Sometimes they appear too restrictive, while the wages of wickedness seem more enticing. We need to ask God to strengthen us and lead us in paths of righteousness.

 God, forgive me for allowing monetary gain and recognition to block out your standards of righteousness. Teach me to walk in holiness.

Consider the guidelines you follow in your life. How do you know which path to follow?

■ A LIVING SACRIFICE

Rom. 12:1-8:   "Therefore, I urge you, brothers, in view of God's mercy, to offer your bodies as living sacrifices, holy and pleasing to God—which is your spiritual worship" (v. 1).

During Old Testament times, animal sacrifices were offered as atonement for sins. We no longer need to present burnt offerings, because Jesus offered himself as the one and final sacrifice for our sins. In response to Jesus' sacrifice for us, we are to offer ourselves as living sacrifices to him.

The trouble with a living sacrifice is that it keeps climbing off the altar. We place ourselves on the altar of God one moment and literally climb off the next moment.

What is the answer to remaining surrendered to God? We need renewed minds, minds that are transformed into thinking from God's perspective, minds that are not influenced by the whispers of the evil one or swayed by secular opinion.

Is it easy to have a transformed mind? Not always. The problem is that we want instant success, instant solutions, with no waiting and void of temptations as a reward for our obedience.

God promises to answer when we call. If we are convinced that God doesn't lie, we will continue to trust God's Word, believing God will answer.

Lord, I offer myself as a living sacrifice for your service today.

The next time you ask God for help, think of a way to serve God too.

■ OUR UNLIMITED DEPOSIT

Heb. 12:1-3: "Let us fix our eyes on Jesus, the author and perfecter of our faith" (v. 2).

Timothy supervises the returns department of a large national bank. Thousands of checks are returned each day for insufficient funds. Many of the same clients overdraw their account month after month.

"Their math skills can't be that bad," Timothy quips. "They must think someone else will deposit funds to their account."

People really are not naive enough to believe that someone will automatically deposit money in their account. However, in our spiritual account with God, each of us has access to an unlimited deposit that enables us to partake of great wealth. The deposit is called faith. Jesus makes the initial deposit of faith within us. We can draw on the deposit without fear of overdrawing, because it comes from the unlimited resources of God. We can continue to apply the deposit to the many situations that demand it. At the same time, it increases in value because Jesus perfects the faith that he has deposited in our hearts.

All this is given as a free gift, but to activate our account of faith requires a simple procedure on our part. The writer of Hebrews admonishes us, "Let us fix our eyes on Jesus." Through him we receive faith to meet all the demands of life.

 Lord, help me to walk by faith to reach my goal.

Consider the generosity of God's unlimited deposit in your account.

■ THE WIPEOUT

1 John 1:5-10:   "If we confess our sins, he is faithful and just and will forgive us our sins and purify us from all unrighteousness" (v. 9).

God had marvelously delivered Tami from a drinking problem. For several months she had not been tempted to return to her weekend partying. Last night, loneliness, coupled with some severe disappointments, weakened her resolve when she was invited to join her old crowd. Alcohol then weakened some of her other resolves.

Marianne's chatter interrupted Tami's self-accusation. "I remember the days before computers, copiers, and correctable typewriter ribbons," Marianne said. "Years ago we typed letters and reports with three carbon copies. If we made one small typing error, it took us ages to correct mistakes."

Tami knew her typing errors could be changed easily. Retyping the correct characters over the wrong ones completely eliminated any record of past errors. Tami wished her sin could be that easily blotted out.

Long before the invention of correctable typewriter ribbons, computers, corrective tape, and correction fluid, Jesus introduced the perfect solution for wiping out sins and mistakes. If we confess our sins, Jesus promises to forgive us and cleanse us of all unrighteousness. His blood blots from God's memory all our past wrongs.

 Jesus, it sounds too easy to simply confess my sins. It seems necessary to wallow in guilt and punish myself. Forgive and cleanse me, O God.

How can you be supportive of your coworkers when they are suffering?

■ SUFFERING

Heb. 5:1-10:   "Although he was a son, he learned obedience from what he suffered" (v. 8).

The mere sound of the word *suffering* causes many to shudder. No one wants to suffer, yet suffering is an integral part of our lives.

Our disobedience often results in suffering, but a deeper meaning of suffering is found in this Bible passage. It means to be made uncomfortable by painfully altering our attitudes and desires. Obedience includes suffering, because it forces us to deny what our flesh desires to do.

Jesus' life was a prime example of this type of suffering. He, of course, never suffered from disobedience, for he was always obedient to his Father. Jesus suffered by denying his own comforts to meet the needs of others. He arose early to pray; he loved the unlovable; he answered the foolish questions meant to trick him. Jesus persevered. He reaped the reward of his suffering. He saw captives set free, the sick healed, his prayer requests answered. He saw joy restored to those who wept. He witnessed truth illuminate those who lived in spiritual darkness. Jesus endured for the joy that was set before him. He knew that suffering was worth the reward.

Because we are God's, our suffering will also reap rewards.

 Jesus, teach me the joy of obedience, the blessing of denying my own desires to meet the needs of others.

Think of a time you saw joy restored in a friend's life.

73

■ PENT-UP EMOTIONS

Eph. 4:25-32:   "Be kind and compassionate to one another, forgiving each other, just as in Christ God forgave you" (v. 32).

Here," Andy said as he slapped a stack of return authorization forms on Dennis's desk. "I didn't have time to finish these. They need to be mailed today."

Dennis glared at Andy's retreating figure. Time after time, Andy passed his work on to Dennis, a fellow manager. A sinister bitterness developed between them. Rather than confront Andy with the source of his anger, Dennis responded with venomous satire.

The anger and resentment that built up within Dennis in a few short weeks threatened to explode in unacceptable behavior. Dennis realized that before he could deal with the problem in a constructive matter and confront Andy objectively he needed to get rid of his anger. But how? Dennis needed a new perspective. His old response maintained that Andy didn't deserve to be forgiven.

Jesus asks us to forgive others not because they deserve it, nor because they will change. He asks us to forgive them as he forgave us.

Dennis knew he didn't deserve God's forgiveness. It was a free gift to him. With this new perspective, Dennis forgave Andy as freely as he had been forgiven.

 Lord of forgiveness, let me follow in your pattern of love.

When a feeling of resentment builds within you, consider offering forgiveness.

◼ REALISTIC EXPECTATIONS

2 Cor. 3:4-6:   "Not that we are competent to claim anything for ourselves, but our competence comes from God" (v. 5).

A new era for Gwen began that September morning after her last child climbed aboard the school bus. After 10 years as a full-time mother the transition was filled with complications. Gwen hadn't realized that office procedures had undergone drastic changes during her absence from the business world. Her typing and accounting skills had withered from lack of use. Office pressures were different than Gwen remembered. All the office personnel in her office complex had 10 to 20 years of experience. Their expertise made Gwen feel even more insecure.

Gwen knew that she certainly could not depend on her own skills alone. She was stripped, shattered, unsure of how to proceed. She recognized that her confidence needed to come from God. Gwen tackled each day with determination, hard work, and faith that God would enable her to become competent.

God did not fail Gwen. It took time. She needed to relax and realize that she could not expect to perform as proficiently as those with senior experience. Realistic expectations coupled with diligent labor enabled Gwen to regain lost skills and learn new procedures.

 Lord, I cling to the belief that you hear me when I pray. I ask that I might become a competent employee.

When you walk in the middle of trouble, remember that God provides insight to overcome the obstacles.

■ RETIREMENT BENEFITS

Rev. 7:9-17: "Never again will they hunger; never again will they thirst" (v. 16).

Social Security was established to assure retired persons income to meet their financial needs, but this government program fails to provide adequate care for those who have retired. Many supplement Social Security payments with additional protection from private savings and programs, especially if their employers do not offer a pension plan.

Mark is one of these. After 40 years of employment with the same company, Mark faced retirement. Mark had been a diligent worker and a faithful employee, but his retirement benefits were inferior when compared with many others.

Circumstances like these show unequal treatment, but God promises equal treatment for all those who call on the name of Jesus. The Bible pictures heaven as a special place, with gold streets and gates of pearl. There we will never again suffer hunger or thirst. Death and sorrow will be past. God himself will wipe the tears from our eyes.

Our most outstanding "retirement benefit" is that after we die we will see Jesus. We shall see him as he really is. We will grasp all that he is and all that he has been to us in the past. The glories of heaven cannot be compared with the glory of God, who fills the heaven with his presence.

 Thank you, God, that you are merciful and just and have a wonderful future planned for us.

Does Jesus outshine all your retirement benefits?

■ GETTING TO KNOW GOD

Dan. 11:27-35:   "But the people that do know their God shall be strong and do exploits" (v. 32 KJV).

Daniel painted a bleak and dreary picture of the future. Yet, interspersed in his picture of doom, are references to the victory that is available to the people that know their God. Not only shall these people remain strong and resist evil; they shall do exploits for God.

This phrase holds the key to experiencing victory in our lives both now and forever: "Get to know God." It is possible to know certain aspects about God, yet, not fully know God. To know God means to believe and trust in his Son Jesus Christ. This relationship with Christ is nurtured through prayer, worship, and reading the Bible.

Nan's opinion of Jean, president of the corporation, has changed. Nan said, "Before I worked as her secretary, I knew Jean's position. I knew certain facts about her life. I saw her as coldly professional with a brilliant, analytical mind." Now Nan realizes that she did not really know Jean Taylor until she had worked as her secretary for five years. Underneath her impressive title, she discovered a warm, caring person who is eager to please others.

When we develop a faith relationship with Christ, we learn to really know God.

 Lord, let me know you—in your humility, love, and glory.

When you are tempted to succumb to doubt, count it as a sign to learn to know God more completely.

■ POLICY AND PROCEDURES

2 Kings 22:8-13:   "Great is the Lord's anger that burns against us because our fathers have not obeyed the words of this book; they have not acted in accordance with all that is written there concerning us" (v. 13).

When Cara became office manager, she inquired about policy and procedures that the company had incorporated. Answers were varied and vague. No one knew where the policy manual was stored. Worse, no one could positively identify rules that had been established. This demonstrates that a policy is not effective just because it exists.

The policy and procedures for God's people are written in the Bible, but this information is beneficial only if it is read and applied.

About 660 B.C. the book of the law given by Moses had been lost. God's rules had been established years earlier, but now the people were ignorant of them and, therefore, unaware of God's requirements and promises. During the reign of the boy king Josiah, the lost book was discovered. When the words were read to King Josiah, he tore his robes in despair. He recognized how greatly they had strayed from God's purposes for them.

Only through the reading of God's book can people learn of God's policy and procedures that will enable them to enjoy his blessings.

 I love your words, O Lord. They bring light to my understanding.

Consider three ways you can learn more about the policies and procedures for God's people.

■ THE PENALTY OF IGNORANCE

2 Kings 22:15-20:   "Because your heart was responsive and you humbled yourself before the Lord" (v. 19).

I can't believe I made that mistake!" Joan fumed. Although Joan did not recall stuffing the letter in the wrong envelope, she realized her error when the irate customer called, maintaining he had not ordered the items that he was being billed for.

King Josiah and the Israelites had innocently disobeyed God. The book of the law had been lost for decades. When judgment was pronounced as a penalty for their wrongdoing, the Israelites could have argued their case with God. First, they could have claimed their disobedience was not really their fault since they had not previously read God's laws. Second, they could have begged for more time to adjust to the law's demands since the message was foreign-sounding, and it takes time to adjust to a newly prescribed way of life. Furthermore, they could have rejected God's words claiming they were too stringent.

But they did not. King Josiah and the Israelites knew they were wrong. This was not a time to procrastinate and push blame on others. It was not a time to refuse to accept responsibility for their failures. It was a time to repent, turn from the past, and live for God.

God was impressed by their responsiveness. Because they wept and humbled themselves, God would extend mercy.

 Lord, I will turn willingly, immediately from my sin.

Have you ever felt humbled by God's generosity?

■ THE REWARD OF KNOWLEDGE

2 Peter 1:1-2:   "Grace and peace be yours in abundance through the knowledge of God and of Jesus our Lord" (v. 2).

When Darlene only partially understood how the computer programs worked in their interfacing of files, she was always a bit uptight when closing a computer job. She feared mistaken commands would wreak havoc with the hidden files by erasing or changing vital information. Gradually she developed an understanding of the transactions, what each program could or could not do, how they affected each other, and the reliability of the commands taken. No longer did she worry that a wrong command would destroy essential information. No longer did her fumbling and confusion cause loss of valuable time. Darlene learned exactly what was expected and the consequences of fulfilling those expectations. The knowledge of the system gave her security in trusting the results to the inner workings of the computer.

In our spiritual life we gain peace through the knowledge of God and of Jesus our Lord. A partial knowledge of God limits the peace that is available to us. As we study God's Word and commune with God, our understanding of God gives us new confidence to overcome every obstacle. This knowledge offers abundant peace that enables us to relax about situations that formerly caused us stress. We know God's purposes and God's promises, which never fail.

 Jesus, Prince of Peace, teach me all the aspects of the peace that is mine through you.

How would you describe the peace God offers?

■ SAFETY PRECAUTIONS

John 17:6-19:   "My prayer is not that you take them out of the world but that you protect them from the evil one" (v. 15).

Across the nation, labor-interest groups are seeking to introduce regulations to protect the health and safety of computer visual-display-terminal users. Reports have indicated physical and emotional stress resulting from the use of VDTs.

Protest groups are not trying to eliminate the VDTs. With precautions, most of the dangers can be eliminated. The protest groups realize that people must be educated to know how to deal with potential risks. As long as companies remain ignorant of the risks, corrective steps will not be taken.

Hazards concern Jesus too. Before he was crucified, his Gethsemane prayer included concern for the spiritual pollution of his present and future followers. "Father," he prayed, "I don't ask that you take them out of the world, but that you keep them from evil."

Isolation from those with different beliefs and life-styles is not the answer. At the same time, many dangers exist that can mar our faith in God. For that, Jesus prayed, "Keep them from evil."

How are we kept from evil? In this Bible reading Jesus explains that we are kept by the power of his name and through the truth of his Word.

 Spirit of truth, protect me from the dangers of the world by the power of your name and the truth of your Word.

Describe a time when you felt protected by the truth of God's Word.

■ EVERYTHING WE NEED

2 Peter 1:3-11:   "His divine power has given us everything we need for life and godliness through our knowledge of him who called us by his own glory and goodness" (v. 3).

Many self-improvement books promise a productive, satisfying life if their principles are followed. Finances, education, or responsibilities often limit our ability in following through their prescribed methods. Even if their principles are followed, the promised results are not always forthcoming.

Long before all these self-help books, God's Word was given to tell us what we need for happiness, fulfillment, and holy lives. The Bible warns us of the dangers that follow if we turn aside from the path of discipleship. God's commands are precise; we do not need to learn by trial-and-error methods. God provides everything we need when temptations confront us.

Many self-help books suggest selfish and unbalanced goals rather than helping others. God's Word tells us how to put on the character of Christ and become well-rounded persons. At the same time, God's instructions for human relationships prevent us from being so heavenly minded that we are of no earthly good.

 Thank you, God, for giving us everything we need for life and godliness.

Think about the seven qualities that 2 Peter tells us to add to our lives: faith, goodness, knowledge, self-control, perseverance, godliness, brotherly kindness, love.

■ PROVISION

1 Kings 17:1-16:   "You will drink from the brook, and I have ordered the ravens to feed you there" (v. 4).

During a three-year drought, God provided food and water for his prophet Elijah. God had instructed Elijah to hide in the Kerith Ravine and to drink from its brook. Ravens brought him bread and meat twice a day. It was supernatural provision from God. Ironically, the brook God had instructed Elijah to drink from soon dried up. It was time for Elijah to move on to new provisions under God's care.

This story exemplifies God's provision for us. He often provides opportunities, occupations, and things to meet our needs. But the provisions aren't ends in themselves. They are not indispensable. Therefore we should not hang on to them, but be open to God's new sources of supply.

Karl found this true in his life. Years earlier he had found a new job that brought him considerable fulfillment. He knew that it had certainly been provided for him by the Lord. Later, the joy in his occupation dissipated. It became a drudgery that sapped his strength and enthusiasm. Yet he felt compelled to continue in the same job, because God had given it to him. Karl needs to understand that God's provisions are stepping-stones to greater heights, not plateaus that limit our climb.

 Lord, make this day new with fresh provision for my needs.

Sort through and discard those things that impede God from providing guidance in your life.

■ TOUCH TYPING

Isa. 6:1-9:   "Then I heard the voice of the Lord saying, 'Whom shall I send? And who will go for us?' And I said, 'Here am I. Send me!' " (v. 8).

Electronic typewriters and word processors have replaced the old manual machines that required steady, uniform pounding. Despite the greatest care, manual typewriters printed erratically and made the typist's fingers tired. Just as typists prefer keyboards with a light touch, God prefers us to be sensitive to the Spirit's touch.

A glimpse of the holiness and glory of the Lord filled Isaiah with dismay and self-loathing. "I am ruined, unclean!" he cried.

Many people initially respond like Isaiah. Their guilt and unworthiness overwhelm them. God does not want us to remain at that point. Isaiah did not. Isaiah's lips were touched, his guilt taken away, his sin removed. No longer did Isaiah see his own inadequacies. Now he saw the Lord. When the Lord inquired, "Whom shall I send to tell the people of me?" Isaiah was prepared. Gratefully, eagerly, he replied, "Here am I, send me!"

We need to see our own failures and inadequacies taken away. We need to see Jesus. When our eyes are off ourselves and on him, we will be filled with the knowledge of God's power to use us. Usually that requires a second, third, or even many more subsequent touches.

 Lord, your touch cleanses me, empowers me, sets me free.

How can you respond to the touch of Jesus?

■ A TIME TO LAUGH

Eccles. 3:1-8:   ". . . a time to weep and a time to laugh" (v. 4).

All morning Hendricks had me sorting through the files," Allison said. "He insisted I misplaced those quotes. You should have seen his face when he found them in his briefcase!" Allison laughed as she recounted the story to her lunchtime friends.

"I could write a book on the trials and tribulations of working for Hendricks," Allison groaned. She mimicked her boss's orders. " 'Type and mail these 10 letters today.' So I do all that and the copier jams, not only jams, but breaks. So I get it fixed. And where is Hendricks to scrawl his mighty signature on them? No one sees hide nor hair of Hendricks until the next day. Did he tell me where he was going?" Allison raises her eyebrows in mock exasperation. "Never!" she answers with a shrug.

Each lunchtime, Allison's soliloquy entertains the lunchroom crew. More importantly, it relieves Allison's stress and the tension of meeting the demands of her eccentric boss.

Although Allison makes fun of Mr. Hendricks, underneath her colorful review of his escapades, her love and respect for him shines through. She finds humor in his antics. Her laughter makes sticky situations tolerable.

Laughter has been proved to lower blood pressure, lessen stress, and improve attitudes. Try it!

 Lord, fill my mouth with laughter. Let me see the humor in tough situations.

The next time you feel frustrated, try laughing about the situation instead of weeping.

■ PASSING PLEASURES

Heb. 11:23-28:   "He chose to be mistreated
along with the people of God rather than to enjoy
the pleasures of sin for a short time" (v. 25).

Be good this weekend," Jessica called to Brad as they
left the office one Friday afternoon.

"Ah," Brad complained, "that's no fun."

Many echo Brad's belief that fun cannot be equated
with being good. "If you don't party or run around,
what do you do for fun?" they ask. Even some
Christians act as if life is dull as they cast longing
glances at the forbidden. Others spend too much time
walking on both sides of the fence. That is a painful
way to walk and not much fun.

Moses grew up in the Egyptian court, which was
notorious for its luxurious life-style. Yet, Moses chose
to lay aside what he found to be only passing pleasures
and follow God, who gives lasting joy.

Partying is only one kind of pleasure, and a
temporary one at that. Past experience for Jessica had
taught her that partying always involved more
anticipation of fun than actual happiness. She kept
hoping for some lasting, dramatic happening to satisfy
the void she felt within. That never happened. Instead
she spent hours drowning out the realities of life,—
finding life as drab as ever the next day.

Jessica discovered that when she found joy and
contentment in Jesus in her everyday living, the need
to drown the weekends in partying lost its appeal.

 Jesus, teach me what real and lasting fun truly
is. Let me not be deceived by superficial
substitutes.

Make a list of lasting sources of joy in your life.

■ COMPANY IMAGE

2 Cor. 5:16-21:   "We are therefore Christ's ambassadors, as though God were making his appeal through us" (v. 20).

When Parke called a local company to confirm an order, the switchboard operator informed him that the company was falling to pieces. "Too many big turkeys around here eating up all the profits," the operator said in a tirade that belittled management and cast doubt on the integrity of the company.

"If it's that bad, why don't you quit?" Parke inquired.

"I will," the operator snapped. Months later she was still there spewing out derogatory comments and poisoning the company's image. Although the operator was efficient in her duties, she was eventually dismissed from her job.

Complaints from critical persons are often unfair and one-sided. Parke advises, "If a company is worth the paycheck you receive, then you owe it respect. If the company is rotten, then quit. Find another job. Don't stay and criticize." Complainers not only reflect a bad image for the company but very often are viewed with suspicion by those who are uncomfortable listening to biased charges.

Just as our words speak for or against the company that employs us, God's reputation, too, depends on those who represent God. We pray, therefore, that we might be good ambassadors of Christ.

 Lord, let me reflect the goodness of your character.

Today build your company's image by the words you speak.

■ THE GREAT PUT-ON

Col. 3:1-10:   "Do not lie to each other, since you have taken off your old self with its practices and have put on the new self, which is being renewed in knowledge in the image of its Creator" (vv. 9-10).

Sure," Mr. Galbre said in response to an inquiry about an overdue bill, "I'll take care of it right away."

Months later Mr. Galbre still had not sent the promised payment. Yet his promises sounded as convincing as ever. "Sorry, you have been more than patient with me. I'll send it this week. I tell everyone that there is not a nicer business to deal with than yours." His voiced sounded as smooth as the plastic telephone receiver that Tiffany held in her hand.

Mr. Galbre brushed aside subsequent calls with the skill of a trained orator. "I admire you," he would say. "You are handling a delicate situation with dignity."

One year later it was obvious that Mr. Galbre's promises were deceptive—a put-on to forestall legal action.

In a recent survey 100 executives of the nation's largest companies listed lying and dishonesty as the most disturbing employee behavior.

In Colossians 3 we are reminded that we have a new self that is being renewed in God's image. Since we have put on that new self, we are to eliminate things that would hinder our new image. We are to strip ourselves of lies, deceit, and falsehood.

 God of truth, rid me of lies, pretenses, and motives that deceive. Clothe me with truth.

Think of ways that you can be more honest on your job.

■ FOLLOWING INSTRUCTIONS

Luke 6:46-49: "Why do you call me, 'Lord, Lord,' and do not do what I say?" (v. 46).

If you have any questions, ask me," Mr. Groff told Bob on his first day of work.

Later, Bob paused, unsure of how to proceed. Gloria, another employee, offered her assistance. She instructed Bob differently than Mr. Groff had done. "Mr. Groff supervises in name only. He never actually does the work. He doesn't know how to do it," she said.

When Mr. Groff noticed the discrepancies in Bob's work, he demanded an explanation. Bob's apologies were weak and shallow. "If you want to last here, listen to my instructions," he informed Bob. "I know what is going on. Gloria constantly attempts to override my policies and undermine my authority. Furthermore, she isn't interested in helping you. The truth is, she constantly misinforms others so that her own mistakes aren't so glaring."

Supervisors aren't always right, but they do have authority. And Bob should have checked what Gloria was saying, with Mr. Groff, before following her advice. Jesus also has authority. The Father gave him "all authority in heaven and on earth" (Matt. 28:18). But unlike earthly supervisors, he does not make mistakes, and we can trust the instructions he gives us. As Jesus' disciples, we need to listen to him and follow his direction.

 Lord, help us to listen to you and to do as you command.

Spend some time reading in the Gospels this week. What do you discover that Jesus is telling you?

89

■ JOB DESCRIPTION

Matt. 28:16-20:   "Go and make disciples of all nations. . ." (v. 19).

Job descriptions enable employees to perform their work effectively. Without them, we would wander about aimlessly, with no clear understanding or description of our tasks.

What kind of job description does God have for you? What is God's intention for you? Some people will tell you, "God has a plan for your life." That is true, but what kind of a plan does God have? Has God chosen the specific person you are to marry? the exact job you are to apply for? the exact place you are to live?

Precious years can go by if we wait for God to reveal a specific roadmap for every aspect of our lives. According to the Bible, God does not always tell us exactly *what* we are to do. More often God tells us *how* we are to live as Christians. Our whole life, actions, attitudes, and vocations should be a positive witness to God's care for us.

There is one job description, though, that God has given to every Christian. Each of us is called to "Go and make disciples of all nations." This specific command from Christ is one of the nonnegotiable parts of our Christian job descriptions.

 Dear God, teach me the kind of attitudes and actions that are consistent with my new life in you.

Give an example of how you could be a witness of God's love at your office.

■ BETRAYING CONFIDENCES

2 Kings 6:8-12:   "Elisha, the prophet who is in
Israel, tells the king of Israel the very words you
speak in your bedroom" (v. 12).

The king of Aram had a problem. During the war he
waged against the Israelites, his army's strategies were
continually uncovered by his opponents. Convinced
that treason lurked within his ranks, the king of Aram
summoned his officers and demanded that the guilty
one confess. The officers pleaded innocence. They
insisted that Elisha, the prophet of Israel, was the
culprit.

The king's initial suspicions of those in his inner
circle are understandable. He knew how easy it is for
people to repeat the contents of private conversations.
In today's business world, employees are often guilty
of confidential, informational leaks. The leaks may
seem innocent of any damaging repercussions, yet
when repeated to a second or third party, the
potential for harm increases.

There are some situations where, as a matter of
conscience, something that is being hushed up should
be brought to the attention of the proper person. But
most of the time God has not given us confidential
information so that we may be an Elisha. It is our
responsibility to respect the confidences of others.

God, give me strength to keep my mouth shut
when I'm tempted to repeat things I should not.
Grant me skill in successfully changing the
subject to more acceptable conversation.

**Make a list of things you can say to build your
company's morale.**

■ DETRACTING ISSUES

2 Cor. 12:7-10:   "There was given me a thorn in my flesh, a messenger of Satan, to torment me" (v. 7).

One autumn, mice invaded the Eaton Furniture Office. Samantha, office manager, detested mice and delegated the project of eliminating mice to the janitor. The janitor set traps and placed poison in strategic places. Each morning the dead remains needed to be removed from the office. Unfortunately, the janitor did not report for work until evening. Samantha requested others to dispose of the carcasses, but they refused. It was not a pleasant job, nor one that is usually required of office workers.

Within each of our occupations lurk things that annoy us. They often are unnecessary burdens.

The apostle Paul suffered a continual thorn from Satan that detracted him from his calling. He prayed to have this messenger of Satan removed. Jesus responded, "My grace is sufficient for you, for my power is made perfect in weakness" (v. 9).

Paul learned that our weaknesses can become our strong points when we draw on God's strength in dealing with them. When we embrace difficulties instead of fighting them, they lose their negative power over us.

 Forgive me, Lord, for complaining about these irritating interruptions that ruin my schedule. Teach me how to turn them into positive experiences.

When you are weakened by heavy burdens, pray for strength from God.

■ KICKBACKS

I Tim. 6:6-16:   "People who want to get rich fall into temptation and a trap and into many foolish and harmful desires that plunge men into ruin and destruction" (v. 9).

Mr. Zarracho aimed for success. His dream was to build a financial empire that would enable him to retire at age 35. As he tried to influence companies to use his services, he discovered the persuasive force of kickbacks. Firms that formerly shunned his services were impressed with the substantial kickbacks that appeared legal and aboveboard. What began as a few sleazy deals enveloped into a full-fledged scam. Mr. Zarracho found the misappropriation of funds and overpayments of fees forced him to create a fictitious firm to handle the kickbacks. His dirty tricks fleeced unsuspecting businesses out of thousands of dollars.

When Mr. Zarracho stood trial for his alleged crimes, he admitted he had not intended to bend the laws as far as he did. It began from the allurement of making a few fast bucks. To cover up those misdeeds required more misconduct.

This is an example of what Paul warned Timothy to avoid. If our goal is riches, we may be plunged into ruin and destruction.

If we choose God as our first desire, God is able to keep money in its rightful place within our lives.

 Lord, I love many of the things money can buy. But more than money and its rewards, I love you. I choose you to be first in my life—always.

What are your most important goals in life?

■ THE CHANGE

Luke 19:1-10:   "For the Son of Man came to seek and to save what was lost" (v. 10).

During lunch breaks Mary sat apart from the other secretaries. With her shoulders hunched over her bowl of soup, she seemed mostly oblivious to the silly stories and small talk that surrounded her. Occasionally, she glanced up. Her eyes, yearning for recognition and acceptance, darted from one to another.

One Sunday Freda's pastor challenged the congregation to pray that all their coworkers would find a relationship with God. Freda tried to dismiss the thought of praying for Mary, because in her eyes Mary was a born loser. Out of obligation, certainly not from concern, Freda included Mary in her prayers.

How can one pray for another and not reach out in love to them? Freda could not. As Freda befriended Mary, she learned that Mary had suffered severe abuse and rejection as a child. Freda's distaste for Mary turned into compassionate understanding. Consequently, Mary blossomed into a new person.

Love has a way of changing people. The Bible character, Zacchaeus, was an outcast. Jesus looked beyond his sin and saw his need. In response to Jesus' companionship, the person others viewed as a sleazy cheat became a respectable community member.

 Lord, wipe out my complacency toward reaching out to those in need. Give me courage to be their friend.

Have you tried to help someone by showing love and acceptance?

■ LISTEN TO ME

Luke 9:37-45:   "Listen carefully to what I am about to tell you: The Son of Man is going to be betrayed into the hands of men" (v. 44).

That was the wrong way to handle it!" the boss yelled at Harold. He criticized Harold not only for his present mistake but for incidents of long ago.

Harold receives much verbal abuse from his employer, but he never grows accustomed to it. "If only he would listen to me," Harold complains. "If he would hear my viewpoint, he could understand why I do what I do."

"Listen to me," is the silent cry of many individuals. Too often we are preoccupied with our own selfish interests and fail to hear the perspective of others.

When Jesus was with his disciples, he often tried to warn them of the impending doom of his crucifixion and the ultimate victory of his resurrection. But his disciples failed to hear. They were too obsessed with the action at hand, too full of their own plans to hear a counter viewpoint.

God desires to talk with us. Too often we cannot hear, for we are busy pounding the gates of heaven with our pleas, trying to convince God of the validity of our viewpoint. Despite our failure to seek to hear God's voice, God sometimes overrides our thoughts with a suggestion, phrase, or Bible verse that clicks with intense clarity. The thought is so vital that we cannot help but recognize it as our Master's voice.

 Speak, Lord, that I may know and do your will.

Find a quiet place where you can listen to God's voice.

■ ROOT PROBLEM

Rom. 3:19-26:   "This righteousness from God comes through faith in Jesus Christ to all who believe" (v. 22).

Get to the root of the problem," Corrine advised. For emphasis, she waved the computer printout in the air. Eric nodded. He had blamed the errors on the sloppy work of his employees. Consequently, each day he had adjusted the figures to conform to the actual count.

By researching the computer programs, Eric pinpointed a program error as the source of the discrepancies. Regardless of the diligence of the computer users, the errors would crop up until the root problem was corrected.

Surface problems are easily spotted. Underlying reasons for them often go undetected. It is the same way with sin. We recognize the symptoms in others. We lash out against immorality, brutality, and pornography. We could rid the world of all these acts, and the root problem would remain a festering evil in God's eyes. The source of these sinful acts is our sinful human natures.

No one is declared righteous in God's sight by obeying laws. Righteousness comes by believing in Jesus Christ, who atones for our wrongdoing. And when we fall in love with Jesus, our actions begin to align with his commandments.

 Lord, you are my living, vital source of wholeness.

How do your actions align with God's commandments?

■ THE VOID

Isa. 55:1-3:   "Why spend money on what is not bread, and your labor on what does not satisfy?" (v. 2).

By itself, a piece of computer hardware is useless. It is simply a piece of electronic machinery waiting to be programmed with instructions and given data to process. And even after all that, the computer only does what it is told to do. It has no desires or motivations of its own.

Human beings are quite different. We are not born into the world as silent pieces of hardware. From the moment we take our first breaths, we make our desires and longings known.

One of the desires God gave us was the craving to be in fellowship with our Creator. Without God's presence in our lives we experience a restlessness that cannot be satisfied by anything else.

We may seek to fill this hunger with excitement, or material things, or people, but substitutes only temporarily satisfy the craving. The void we feel may be pushed temporarily into the background of our subconscious. We may be distracted, but we will never be content until we find that Jesus satisfies our need.

 Remind me, Lord, of my constant need for you.

Avoid meaningless, frantic activity. Instead, build a relationship with the One who loves you most.

■ WHY PRAY?

Mark 10:46-52:   " 'What do you want me to do for you?' Jesus asked him" (v. 51).

Bartimaeus cried out, "Jesus, Son of David, have mercy on me!" He had heard of Jesus healing others, and he longed to receive his sight. When the crowds, angered by Bartimaeus' disruptive behavior, ordered him to be quiet, Bartimaeus cried even louder to the One he knew could help him.

Jesus asked Bartimaeus, "What do you want me to do for you?" Certainly, the all-knowing God knew Bartimaeus' answer and could even see the reason as the blind beggar stood before him. But Jesus wanted him to verbalize his requests.

Articulating our requests is more for our own benefit than God's. When we translate our thoughts into prayers, we need to sort out the confusion that clutters our minds and concentrate on what we really desire God to do.

Prayer is both the easiest and the most difficult activity in the world. All we need to do is open our mouths, say a few words, and watch God do it. Simple, isn't it? Yet countless times we wrestle with finding the time and energy to do that. Why? Because Satan knows the power of prayer. He brings his whole host of opposition to halt this power source.

When we pray, there is power in the name of Jesus. In order to change situations, release faith in his name.

God, prayer is a privilege. It is powerful. Give me the urge to pray, and the discipline to pray.

Begin today to make a habit of praying for each of your coworkers.

■ WORK, A CURSE OR A BLESSING?

Gen. 2:8-15:   "The Lord God took the man and put him in the Garden of Eden to work it and take care of it" (v. 15).

If only Adam and Eve would not have eaten the apple, then we wouldn't need to be slaving here," Jerry complained. But work is not a curse caused by Adam and Eve's sin. God had given Adam the responsibility of tending the Garden of Eden long before the fall. The resultant curse did rob labor of its joy, but that does not mean we can have no joy in labor. Jesus has redeemed us from the curse. His presence restores the purpose of labor to God's original design.

Completed duties give us the satisfaction of a job well done. Jobs add order, purpose, and meaning to our lives. As we meet our duties, self-pity and depression are forced to flee. Work prevents idleness, which often breeds jealousy, gossip, and wickedness. Rest and recreation are even more pleasurable as a temporary respite from our careers.

Our enjoyment of our job does not depend so much on the type of job we have as on our attitude toward it. If we daily recognize the positive effects of our employment, we will enjoy our labor.

 Father, thank you for a sound mind and a strong body that allow me the opportunity to work, to earn a livelihood and become successful.

If you could choose a new career, what would you choose and why?

■ TIME MANAGEMENT

Prov. 24:3-14:   "By wisdom a house is built, and through understanding it is established" (v. 3).

Jill had a vague unrest that things were out of control in her life. It was a pressing frustration of too much to do and not enough time. Managing both home and office required remembering details to keep both running smoothly. Jill always had an obscure feeling of something forgotten or unfinished nagging her.

To solve the unrest and to manage both home and office more effectively, Jill learned to list every day's duties. When everything was mapped out on paper, she could juggle the duties to fit the time limits she had. She learned to set realistic time limits. She no longer worries that she has forgotten an appointment, because it is always written down in advance.

Crossing off a completed activity gives Jill a sense of achievement. With all her duties clearly listed, she analyzes the best way and time to complete a goal. She forces herself to finish each duty whether she feels like it or not.

"It seems like I have more time now," Jill says. A written list frees the mind from its frantic pace of trying to recall details. The mind is more capable of concentrating on the task at hand.

 Lord, thank you that you never put more responsibility on me than you allow time to meet those needs.

Keep a two-day record of how you spend your day at work and home. Do you try to squeeze too much into too little time?

■ SELF-GRATIFICATION

Matt. 4:1-11:   "Man does not live on bread alone, but on every word that comes from the mouth of God" (v. 4).

After his baptism in the Jordan River, Jesus was led by the Spirit into the desert. Jesus' ministry was only beginning. This was a time of solitary seeking to clearly hear God's direction for his future. After 40 days and nights of prayer and fasting, Jesus was hungry.

"If you are the Son of God," Satan mocked him, "turn these stones into bread." There is no commandment that we should not turn stones into bread. It was not the act itself that was wrong. It was the instigator behind the challenge who made it wrong. Satan knew that Jesus was ready to launch into a ministry that would weaken Satan's own strength and influence over others. If Jesus became preoccupied with his own desires, he would take his eyes off his true calling of helping others.

Self-gratification robs us of needed energy to meet the needs of those we are called to serve. If we yield to it, we waste time and energy on taking care of ourselves and have little or no time to help others.

Jesus consistently combated his temptations with Scripture. In the end the devil left him, and angels came and ministered unto him.

 Lord, meeting my own needs first is not only selfish in your eyes, it is lonely, unrewarding, and empty for me.

Make Bible reading a part of each day.

■ GOAL SETTING

Phil. 3:12-16:   "I press on toward the goal . . ."
(v. 14).

A goal is something we hope to achieve but have not yet attained. Goals are risky. They provide us with direction and aim, yet we take a chance in investing time and energy with no guarantee that we will achieve our dreams.

To some extent, goals limit our options. They require us to eliminate other interesting possibilities. But when we are able to make a choice and set our sights on one goal, we build a stronger foundation than we would by trying to do everything at once.

Linda discovered the cost of committing herself to the goal of becoming a business investor. To pursue it she needed to forego tennis tournaments and her needlecraft. She would have to study for some years and try to climb up from the bottom, competing in a male-dominated field.

Linda had no promise that her perseverance would lead to her goal. But she did not give up. When other opportunities presented themselves, she would review her goals. A clearly defined statement of her goals helped her to achieve many of them.

There is one goal in particular, though, that we should have at the top of our list. Like Paul, we should set our sights first on the upward call of Jesus.

 Dear God, help me set realistic goals that are pleasing to you, and enable me to pursue them diligently.

Think of the goals you set. How has God provided you direction?

■ PEER PRESSURE

John 9:1-34:   "The man answered, "Now that is remarkable! You don't know where he comes from, yet he opened my eyes" (v. 30).

How can someone who tries so hard, fail so often?" Joyce asked. "I go to church, read the Bible, and pray, yet I continually compromise my beliefs and follow the office crowd."

Joyce's problem is not unique. She means well, and she begins her day with good intentions. She ends her day praying for forgiveness. In between she fails.

In the Bible reading for today, we learn how Jesus healed a blind man. The leaders tried to convince the formerly blind man to deny that Jesus was the Son of God. Hours of grueling questions, accusations, and ridicule did not destroy the man's faith. Instead, his faith increased.

Today few of us are taken before church councils and governments and asked to recant our beliefs, but every day we are faced with a question: will we live for God, or will we compromise?

It is during these times of temptation that we need to draw spiritual strength to remain firm in our beliefs. It is not a time to concentrate on do's and don'ts. It is a time to be inwardly aware of the past and present goodness of Jesus and of his future promises. Through the power of God's Holy Spirit we no longer need to be on the defensive. Jesus makes us victorious!

 O God, make me strong for you. Let me be a giver of your love.

Today fill your thoughts with the goodness of Jesus.

■ LET US NOT GIVE UP

Heb. 10:19-25:   "Let us not give up meeting together, as some are in the habit of doing" (v. 25).

Replacing their manual system with a computerized one completely changed everyone's methods at Cooper Company. The change required months of overtime and additional temporary help. Mistakes, corrections, revisions, and changes seemed endless.

Within the year the agony of the transition had faded. The computerized system really did turn out to be more efficient and less costly. The trials of earlier months no longer plagued employees. No one in the office desired to return to the former manual system.

"Funny," Josh muses, "but that experience taught me a spiritual truth. I had stopped going to Sunday morning church services. Getting up early, dressing the kids, and racing to the services didn't seem to be worth the hassle to either my wife or me. Exhausted, we would collapse into a pew, nursing our anger at the bitter accusations we had hurled at each other while driving to church.

"When I experienced the benefits after we had adjusted to the computer at work, I thought that perhaps we needed time to get ready for church. Together, my wife and I found ways to make Sunday morning preparations easier on our nerves. It required some planning, but now our whole family enjoys church. Our preparations have settled into a fairly calm routine."

Lord, forgive me when I place a higher priority on preparing for work than preparing to worship you.

How do you prepare for worship?

■ FORGOTTEN PRINCIPLES

Gal. 4:8-20:   "But now that you know God—or rather are known by God—how is it that you are turning back to those weak and miserable principles?" (v. 9).

Lois attended a three-day seminar on effective management. On her first day back at work, she found a backlog of problems which required immediate attention. Next she became absorbed in a stack of unopened mail on her desk. At the end of her day she stuck the seminar's manual on her bookshelf, intending to study it more thoroughly later. Unfortunately, Lois forgot the principles she learned but never practiced. Nothing positive resulted from the seminar's teaching for either Lois or for those working under her management.

As Christians we face the same dilemma, but this waste of knowledge need not happen. If we harness our actions to conform to our desires, we can retain the insights we learn from sermons, speakers, or books. Write down the concepts. Set aside time each day to read, meditate, and develop new insights. Plan constructive action in following through with them. Pray that the Holy Spirit will make the new understanding a part of you.

 Lord, you opened the windows of my mind to grasp new insight. Teach me to apply it to my life.

Think of a way you can put into practice a lesson learned in a sermon or seminar.

■ LET IT REST

Phil. 4:4-9:   "Do not be anxious about anything, but in everything by prayer and petition, with thanksgiving, present your requests to God" (v. 6).

Marj added the accounts receivable. The total did not agree with the entered cash amount on the computer printout. Eventually time forced her to lay aside the unfinished task and perform her remaining duties. But the cash discrepancy nagged at her and prevented her from fully concentrating on billing customers. The preoccupation with her unfinished task caused mistakes in her other work. After repeatedly correcting stupid mistakes, Marj forced her mind to lay aside the nagging problem and concentrate fully on her task at hand.

Experience teaches us that we can work more effectively when we free our mind of conflicting ideas and concentrate on our present duty. Sometimes we believe we need a drastic intervention of God's power to bring peace to our minds. Frantically we beg God for some divine action. In a daze we perform the most basic functions, yet we are totally preoccupied with our problem.

God has an antidote to this problem. God invites us not to be anxious, but to request God's help and give thanks in advance for it. True, it isn't the easiest advice to follow when we are familiar with indulging in worry, but God does not request more from us than God gives us strength to perform.

 Lord, help me to trust in your unfailing care.

Force yourself to concentrate on one task at a time.

■ WHO IS SUCCESSFUL?

LET IT REST

Ps. 1:1-6:   "He is like a tree planted by streams of water, which yields its fruit in season and whose leaf does not wither. Whatever he does prospers" (v. 3).

Who is successful? Is it one who achieves position, wealth, or fame? Is it the person who accomplishes his or her goals? Some people set low goals that are easy to achieve. Others set impossible goals that are never reached, yet they accomplish far more than those with lesser standards.

According to the Word of God, success is reaching the potential God has planned for us. Our Bible reading for today promises prosperity for those who place their trust in God. Does that imply that success is synonymous with financial prosperity? We all have heard of wealthy individuals, weighted by depression, who committed suicide. How could that be termed success? God promises prosperity to the one who delights in God's law. That person is compared to a tree that yields fruit in its season. Whatever this person does will prosper, because by meditating on God's Word the person will embark only on those plans that align with God's will.

We should not try to judge the success of another. Instead, let us concentrate on living up to the potential God intends for us.

 Lord, teach me how to prosper in all that you have planned for me.

What is your definition of success?

■ FINISHING THE RACE

2 Tim. 4:1-8:   "Now there is in store for me the crown of righteousness, which the Lord, the righteous Judge, will award to me on that day—and not only to me, but also to all who have longed for his appearing" (v. 8).

In honor of Perry's 30 years of service as president of a multimillion-dollar business, a retirement celebration was held. Among those present was Jennifer, an eager junior executive. As she shook Perry's hand, she said, "I hope that I will be as lucky as you and someday be president of this company."

The old gentleman put his hand on the young executive's shoulder and said, "Jennifer, luck isn't part of the package for success. If you want to reach the top, you work at the bottom, not only when you feel like it—but always. Be continually on the lookout for improvements, correct mistakes, and never expect more of others than you are willing to give yourself. Don't consider others as competition, but as team members whom you need to achieve your goals."

In our Bible reading we find almost identical advice given to Timothy from Paul, a veteran follower of Christ: "Be prepared in season and out of season; correct, rebuke and encourage—with great patience and careful instruction" (v. 2). We, too, can follow this advice, and the final goal—life with Christ, complete with a crown of righteousness—will be ours.

 Lord, when I have finished the work you planned for me, may I say like apostle Paul: "I have fought the good fight, I have finished the race, I have kept the faith."

Enjoy finishing the race with Jesus by your side.

BIBLE READINGS SERIES

Bible Readings for Men
Steve Swanson

Bible Readings for the Retired
Leslie F. Brandt

Bible Readings for Couples
Margaret and Erling Wold

Bible Readings for Parents
Ron and Lyn Klug

Bible Readings for Teachers
Ruth Stenerson

Bible Readings for Singles
Ruth Stenerson

Bible Readings for Teenagers
Charles S. Mueller

Bible Readings for Families
Mildred and Luverne Tengbom

Bible Readings for Farm Living
Frederick Baltz

Bible Readings for Troubled Times
Leslie F. Brandt

Bible Readings for Growing Christians
Kevin E. Ruffcorn

Bible Readings for Church Workers
Harry N. Huxhold

Bible Readings for Women
Lyn Klug

Bible Readings for Mothers
Mildred Tengbom